Landscape of Loss

Cover photo: Kitchen Mesa on Ghost Ranch near Abiquiu, New Mexico
Photo credit: Eugene Blake
Book design: Jackie Kerr

Landscape of Loss

My Grief Journey

by Sherry A. Phillips

with reflections by the Rev. Eugene Blake

Dedication

This book is dedicated to my sons and their families:
Shane and Shelley plus Derek and Abby in Texas;
Jason and Kristen plus Krystine, Hannah and AnnMarie here in Kansas.
Their loss is as great as mine; even more so for Hannah and AnnMarie
who never had the chance to know their Papa
except through memories we share.

Roy's mother, Ruth, has my deepest appreciation.
We have been a source of strength and inspiration for each other.

To my sister, Sheryl, who began to traverse this rutted road of loss
when her husband, Frank, died of cancer. She was forty years of age
with three sons: Chuck, Steve, and Ed.

And to my longtime friend, Gene Blake,
who with patience and wisdom was willing to journey with me.

Thank you to Ina Hughes for the writing tools necessary
for me to put my journey on paper.

Table of Contents

Introduction	9
The Day Roy Died	13
Bittersweet Memories	15
Spiral-Bound Memory With a Red Cover	17
My Challenge	20
Life Together	24
Butterfly	27
I Am Sorry for Your Loss	29
A Contemporary Psalm of Lament	30
Rude Awakening to Anger	32
Hugging Helps	34
The Significance of Sexual Love	38
Dust	38
Is That You Babe?	42
Excuses for not Writing	43
This Is no Picnic	45
Anniversaries	48
Get Some Boots	55
Christmas Without Papa	56
Icy Obstacles	58
My First-Born Son	61
What Shall I Send?	63
A Goodbye Letter	67
Damn You, Roy Richard Phillips	69
An End to the First Year	74
Reminders	77

This Day Is too Hard	78
Is This Normal?	79
Pickup	81
Twenty Months	84
Widow Woes: A Chronicle	86
A Time for Everything	88
Memories Found in a Bottom Drawer	92
How Ya' Doin'?	95
Ebb and Flow	99
One Step	102
What Comes Next?	103
Red Roses	105
Waiting	108
It's About Time	111
Krystine and Three Trees	111
The Next Days	113
Life Lessons From the Landscape	115
Finding Peace: Another Lesson	119
Some Things Never Change	121
Treasure Island	122
Happy New Year to Me – Chinese That Is!	123
This Time Is for Me	126
Turning to the Future	129
We Remember Dad	131
Dedicated to Gardeners Everywhere	132
The Old Oak by Eugene Blake	135
Sherry Phillips Reflects With Testimony to Life	138
Tortoise Wins the Race of her Life	139
Perseverance	140
About the Authors	142

Introduction

The fall from the pinnacle of my life was like stepping on loose stones at the edge of a steep chasm and becoming part of a rock slide. Slipping down the mountain; landing broken, bruised and bleeding on a rough boulder-strewn road. I could assume the road would lead somewhere. But I had no map. Grief following sudden death begins an agonizing journey.

My husband, Roy Richard Phillips, died in the backyard of our home on South Estelle in southeast Wichita, Kansas, March 23, 2002. He had just turned 59. Married for not quite 39 years we were already planning our 40th wedding anniversary trip to the Netherlands.

This collection of thoughts and feelings describes many of my challenges stumbling along the scary unmarked road called grief. Writing became a therapy to help me struggle through the wilderness of loss to discover life in the garden of my existence.

These stories of my trek over pock-marked landscape through dark days are written for me and maybe you. The reflections are of my experiences with horrendous grief but everyone encounters loss. Memories of Roy and our life together were gifts to help me accept his death. It made for slow going.

I wanted to record what happened after I found Roy half-sitting, half-lying on the south side of the backyard next to the chain link fence. I needed to explain what happened from the time we got out of bed that morning until I found him at 3:30 that afternoon. I was afraid I would lose my mind, lose the precious memories stored there. It felt like awakening from a deep sleep and realizing your dream is slipping away.

I continued to write because I had special memories of Roy to share. Hannah, the youngest grandchild, was only three-and-a-half months old when the Papa, whom she would never remember knowing, died. The other three grandchildren, Derek, almost seven, his sister, Abby, age three, and Hannah's big sister, Krystine, soon to be five, were all too young to understand the sudden death of their grandfather – their Papa.

Writing of the ebony nights of my grief reawakened my senses enabling me to feel, to see, to hear again in the morning bright of a new day. It's more than survival or setting daily goals; it's learning to live alone without being lonely, being able to laugh again.

Roy fell dead while mowing. He had worked for almost four hours doing early spring cleanup of the yard. It was the Saturday afternoon before Palm Sunday. The following days of spring gave witness that my life did not end with his. Elderberry bushes grew into a jungle of branches and bloomed into dinner plate size canopies of china white blossoms. Growing along the fence where I had found Roy lying, the bushes stretched up eight feet into a sun-bleached blue sky. They seemed to grow in defiance of his spring chopping. Bermuda grass greened, and I marveled that anything could go on living that hot, dry summer.

The opportunity to learn the mechanics and soul of writing began with what I see now as God's plan to help me live through my devastating loss.

In January, I had made a promise to my long-time friend, Gene Blake, to drive with him to the Ghost Ranch Conference and Retreat Center of the Presbyterian Church (U.S.A.) at Abiquiu, New Mexico. Gene had signed up to take a weeklong workshop to work on his writing skills. His disability episodes grip him with overwhelming tiredness. He had asked me to go along. It was an assurance he could get to Ghost Ranch safely.

As one of my closest friends, I knew he would help me deal with the emotional upheaval of Roy's death. Gene and his wife, Mary, drove from their home in Winfield, Kansas, as soon as they got the call about Roy dying.

As a church pastor, Gene's experience in ministry included grief and divorce support counseling. He cares and has the patience to understand the depth and breadth of emotional upheaval.

The treasure of sunset and sunrise that cradled the bright blue skies of early May as we drove west seemed to swallow my questions of "why?" and "why now?" Even in such desperate hours I felt like God would not leave me alone in that place called grief. It felt like when I was a child being held close in my mother's arms.

During that week in the writing class, I began to learn how to put my grief on blank paper. I was in a community of caring strangers tutored by a sensitive instructor with a hearty sense of humor. Ina Hughs, columnist for the *Knoxville News Sentinel* in Knoxville, Tennessee, taught us a variety of ways to tell our stories. She spread out an array of tools that would help me work the ground of my future.

I felt such a compulsion to tell over and over again the story of Roy's dying. But the listing and repetition style of writing creative non-fiction opened up a way to tell the stories about Roy and me. *Life Together* was the beginning of a series of experiences I have written about in order to share Roy, our life and my grief with others.

That twelve-hour drive over two days was the first time I left the last place where I had been held in Roy's arms. Leaving and returning alone to our home of over 30 years encompassed agonizing experiences. Feelings I could not name swallowed me like a violent ocean yet my body felt like I was no more than a mirage in the desert struggling against a sandstorm. That journey to Ghost Ranch would become for me a template for my trek across a barren, wide-open space with a horizon too far away to reach.

In spite of the reality of Roy's death, all along the rocky path my feet had been set upon I found the gifts of living. With the help of family and friendships I would learn to see and hear and feel the goodness of life again.

In the fence-to-fence Bermuda green of backyard, a free flowing river of cedar mulched landscape now eases the memory of death too soon. The life cycle of lavender hosta, blue hydrangea, purple salvia, pink creeping roses and rich gold daylilies give testimony that life goes on. Mock orange, red twig dogwood, and gold mound spirea are tucked under Snow crab, Forest Pansy redbud, Canadian cherry, Canarti juniper, and Amur maple trees. The flamenco dance of butterflies and busy buzz of bumblebees, accompanied by song from wren and robin, render mute the crash, rattle, bang in my head. My heart and mind, once gripped in fear of facing each overwhelming day, are strong once more.

God has refused to allow my long walk in the darkness of my bereaved soul to have no end. The surprises of color have splashed me with newness – a future symbolic of resurrection and transformation – Roy's and mine. These are the stories of my growing.

The Day Roy Died

That Saturday started with a two-hour rehearsal of the Mt. Vernon Presbyterian Church choir for the Palm Sunday cantata they would sing the next day. Roy sang bass and he had practiced at home and in the car but I had not heard any of the music. Or maybe I just didn't listen.

After practice, about noon, Roy returned home with the need to eat a quick lunch and start his pre-planned four hours of early spring yard work. I was to run Saturday errands – drop off recycles and then to Town West Mall to shop for cards for all of the birthdays and anniversaries coming up in the next few months.

Roy was a planned-man. The Wichita State University Shocker baseball team was playing out of town at Evansville at 2:00 p.m. so he had put on his Sony Walkman headset, his facemask to filter the heavy dust that would cover grass and leaves. He had on his straw hat, the one with the Missouri Valley Conference college names and logos, to shade his face from the very warm March sun.

It appeared everything on his schedule had been done except to finish mowing the backyard, take a quick shower and rest before we were to meet our younger son Jason, wife, Kristen, and granddaughters Krystine and Hannah for dinner.

When I found Roy, soon after I got home about 3:30 p.m., the EMS crew said it didn't look good. While they gave him CPR and inserted a breathing tube, I was busy calling Jason, and Roy's folks to meet us at the hospital. I called my sister Sheryl telling her to call our pastor. "Roy collapsed in the yard and we're on the way to St. Joseph Hospital." Thank God she thought to call our sister, Barbara, brother, Bill and our dad, Gene Hager.

Jason drove up as they lifted the gurney into the ambulance. At 4 p.m. still in front of the house, the EMS tech stepped back out of the ambulance to say they were in touch with the hospital. Another tech opened the door and told us Roy was dead. Jason and I looked at each other stunned and began to cry. We drove on to the hospital to tell everyone that our Roy was gone. Shock, disbelief and the inevitable questions, confronted us. As we held each other, a chaplain led us to a quiet room with a phone. Through tears I told everyone what little I knew.

I tried to call our older son Shane. He and Shelley and the kids were on vacation somewhere in Texas. Roy's sister Anne needed to be told in person so Roy's folks left for the Needle Nook Fabric Shop she owned before Saturday closing to break the news. Her predicted collapse upon hearing of the death of her beloved older brother was met with arms to fall into. The folks went on home to call Roy's brothers – Ronnie here in Wichita, Robert in Washington, and Russell in Oregon.

Pastor Dennis Winzenreid would call the choir members. Would they, could they, sing that cantata tomorrow?

Shane called home about 7:00 p.m. after hearing our urgent messages left on his voice mail. He apologized for missing my calls – they had been swimming all afternoon and then gone to get a bite to eat. His cell phone had been left in the hotel room. It was horrible to tell him on the phone. He was so far away to have to hear me say, "Your dad collapsed in the yard and died late this afternoon." I heard his disbelieving voice with choked back sobs say to Shelley and the kids, "Dad's dead?"

I encouraged them to leave for Flower Mound early the next morning, then re-pack and come on to Wichita early Monday. "We'll be okay. Call me when you get home."

My memories of that evening are vivid like watching a rerun. But the sounds of people in the dining room coming in with tears, hugs and mumbled words of condolence and disbelief are a blur. Phone calls were made. I talked with Roy's secretary, Marty. It would be up to her to contact Roy's boss, Jack Pelton, and others at Cessna Aircraft Company.

After everyone was gone, except Jason who stayed with me overnight, I crawled onto my bed alone for the first time – a widow.

Bittersweet Memories

The plans were familiar, even routine. He would arrive home on Friday at 5 p.m. She would have hair combed, lipstick freshened, purse in hand and be waiting for the honk of his horn.

Out the back door, through the garage she jumped into the car with, "Hi, Babe!"

"Hi Babe, where shall we go?" was his predictable response.

"I don't care – really. How about the Cactus Cantina? Feel like a strawberry margarita? There's a movie I'd like to see."

"Let's do it!" And the car would back down the driveway.

This scene would vary only a little that last Friday night. Earlier in the afternoon Mimi had agreed to watch the two grand-girls for a few hours between son dropping them off and daughter-in-law picking them up. Baby Hannah had cried herself to sleep accompanied by a bottle of milk prepared by her daddy and a soft song from Mimi. Big sister, Miss Krystine, sat on the floor drawing and coloring pictures using the new tote box as a desktop. At almost five, she was big enough to be helpful.

Krystine was the first to hear the garage door go up, the back door slam and Papa's boots coming across the office-dining room tile. "Papa's home!" she shouted and jumped up to run meet him. Baby Hannah woke with a start and began a wailing that made big tears flow down each cheek.

Papa stooped to pick up K.P. and "bear hug" her. Krystine's laughter turned to happy chatter. Mimi tried to console Hannah who, at three-and-a-half months had no idea what wonderful things were happening. All the while the small green bedroom almost burst with shrieks and laughter as happiness exploded. Yes, Babe, a.k.a. Roy or Papa, was home and early.

Setting Krystine down he listened to her monologue about art and other busyness. Then he reached down with his large mechanic-plumber-carpenter turned engineering director hands and scooped Hannah up from my shoulder. Sitting down beside me on the loveseat size couch he rolled her over so that her back now lay like a hot dog in a bun in his left hand. With his right hand free he began his infamous foot massage. Even at her tender age she responded to the gentle pressure of fingers and thumb. At the same time, Papa's left hand was massaging Baby Hannah's back. His gentle caresses and quiet voice began to calm our startled bundle of joy. I went in search of the camera.

The girls' mom entered through the open garage door apologizing for being late and keeping us from dinner. My smile reassured her that our familiar routine could wait while this special moment in time was captured forever.

A few quick pictures – the one of Papa, a not-yet quieted Baby Hannah, and Mom Kristen with K.P. peaking between shoulders captured the sweetness of a brief moment in time.

It wasn't until the film was developed along with the other 35mm rolls taken of flowers, visitors and family gathered for Roy's funeral that the 5 p.m. Friday moments the evening before he died were revisited.

As soon as the girls headed home that last Friday night, Babe and I had jumped into the car and drove south for dinner at romantic Marbella Restaurant on the north side of little city Derby. Strawberry margaritas would be replaced with iced tea flavored with lemon and two packets of Sweet 'n Low and a scrumptious dinner buffet of salmon filet. Dessert of white Zinfandel and coffee was accompanied by small talk, hand holding and smiling eyes that traded loving glances.

Trying to catch an early movie at the Derby Cinema was more often to be ahead of the pre-teen and date crowd than to take advantage of the "all movies before six o'clock discount." Although this Director of Systems Integration and Design for Cessna Aircraft Company and his peace-and-justice advocate wife of almost 39 years were known to appreciate the savings made available to seniors and others. Living wisely was the term often used.

We liked first released movies and *Ice Age* would have us talking on the way home about the animation and sophisticated dialogue. This movie made a statement about cooperation and addressing injustice but the story was more for grownups than kids. It entertained but we wondered whether "they" would get it.

Our life had been full of goodness. It was satisfying, complete, purposeful, spontaneous, and planned. There were the two marvelous sons, Shane and Jason, and our terrific daughters-in-law, Shelley and Kristen. Then came the four children we called grand, as well as, Derek, Abigail (Abby), Krystine (Miss K.P.) and Hannah.

At this writing in August 2002, Roy's folks, Ruth and Ray, are alive. So are my dad, Gene Hager, and his wife, Lil. We have three sisters and four brothers between us. Our planning for the end of life had been intentional. Since I was diagnosed as a type I diabetic when I was 19 we never thought Roy would die first.

The only thing God promised was that we would have choices. Roy and I made choices that were sometimes questionable. Our life had predictable challenges and some hard times. But I will always remember our life together was more like enjoying giant-sized Route 44 diet cherry limeades from Sonic and listening to *Celebration* sung by Kool and the Gang with the bass turned full up.

Spiral-Bound Memory With a Red Cover

She spoke with hesitation as she approached me at the coffee and punch table after morning worship, "I don't mean to be bothering you, Sherry. I know this is a tough time. The last thing you need to hear is a lot of advice from everyone. I don't want to do that. I just wanted to share with you what I thought was a good idea from a friend of mine. I found this to be very helpful when my husband died."

"That's kind of you," I mumbled in a hollow voice as we moved away from the line of thirsty congregants with our foam cups. I had been offered lots of advice in the first weeks after Roy's death. I remember thinking, "I won't remember what she says."

Kathleen went on to say that her friend had told her about getting a spiral-bound notebook to record everything she did after her husband's death. "You can get one with a bright colored cover – something easy to see in the stacks of mail and confusion that collects in a crisis. I wrote everything down in that notebook."

She said that it was easy to thumb back through the notebook to track what had to be done. With the date noted it was easy to see what needed follow up. It was diary, log, and to-do list. Memory bound into a file that would replace notepads and backs of envelopes. "You can put anything into it you want. And if you fill it up you can always get another one. I didn't even worry about keeping it in any order. Anything I didn't want to forget I wrote down in that notebook."

I gave Kathleen a smile and squeezed her hand – my way of saying thanks. Then after lunch I drove over to Wal-Mart.

Gene Blake reflects

When Sherry and I decided to write this book, one of our priorities was to refrain from advice giving. People who grieve the loss of a loved one get plenty of advice – most of which is unwanted, insensitive, and inappropriate. There is a common human desire to be helpful in a hurtful situation. But there are no magic statements, no great words of wisdom, to heal a broken heart. Usually, what the bereaved find most helpful is a person's mere presence and ability to listen.

The widow who approached Sherry at church did so with reservation and humility. She too, had once received a lot of advice. Yet there was one suggestion she'd found helpful and was moved to share. It is also the one piece of advice Sherry desires to share.

Business matters that must be dealt with are an overwhelming reality of grief. These are particularly difficult when one is in a state of shock. There are death benefits to be applied for, names to be removed from or added to lists, responsibilities once shouldered by a spouse that must now be assumed. The list can seem endless, and one's memory is suffering too. Written reminders can prove to be of great benefit.

Sherry did purchase a spiral-bound notebook and used it to record the following:

- Benefits due and received,
- Expenditure estimates for determining income needs,
- Significant expenses paid – to whom, how much, and when,
- Account numbers, PIN numbers, and passwords,
- List of expenses Roy had paid annually and semi-annually,
- Dates of meetings with her attorney and financial planner along with a summary of the meeting,
- Who was contacted about removing Roy's name from business records,
- Names and phone numbers of contacts with Roy's employer concerning questions about benefits.

She even copied all of Roy's business papers and computer reports and tucked them between the covers.

In a separate notebook she accumulated lists of cards, visitors, food, etc. This served as a helpful reminder of the ways concern had been shown by family and friends. The lists also aided her as she wrote thank-you notes.

Recording names, dates, expenses, to-do lists, decisions, reminders, etc. in a spiral-bound notebook is something Sherry and her church friend found to be quite helpful. Of course, it's a suggestion each individual can adapt to her or his own needs.

There's another way a notebook can be helpful. For some the process of journaling – writing about feelings, frustrations, and experiences – is a healing process. Later, when rereading their journal, they can also gauge the progress they've made. People who are not comfortable talking about their grief, or don't have a good listener handy, but have even marginal writing skills, can make that trip to Wal-Mart and create a spiral-bound memory book. And, yes, red's a good color. ❃

My Challenge

Friday night early May 2002
Saying "yes" to a faithful friend was easy in January. Now my mind doubts. I must pack. Gene Blake picks me up tomorrow. The cold feeling of aloneness makes me shiver. I feel like a baby left on the doorstep of a convent.

Helping Gene drive to Ghost Ranch means leaving Roy's spirit in the backyard where he died in March. I know it's crazy but I just can't shake this feeling. Is Roy standing by the chain link fence on the south side where he fell? He seems to be waiting.

I say out loud, "Stop this crazy talk and pack!"

Saturday morning
My promise to a friend is the only force that makes me zip this bag and set it by the front door to wait. Gene will understand my challenge just as I have understood his challenge these last several years. He will accept my tears and fears. He will listen and be a source of courage for me to face what comes. Even with his disability he is like a rock. Trusted friend. Wise counselor.

Early Saturday afternoon
Gene points to a box of Kleenex and says, "Just in case." His usual pack of sugar free chewing gum, cheese crackers, and the map are here in the seat. He is ready to go and knows I am not. We head west on Highway 54 for northern New Mexico.

Gene is always prepared. He wants me sitting in the seat beside him ready to take over the driving if needed. Gene isn't afraid of having a disability episode of body-numbing, mind-dulling fatigue; he just doesn't want to have one while driving by himself somewhere in the middle of anywhere. With another driver, he can begin the necessary sleep cycle to get through his continual threat until a bed is found.

Saturday evening after supper in western Kansas
Gene says, "After we get settled in our rooms at the motel what say we go get something to drink?"

My numbness was beginning to prickle when I answered, "Great and maybe a short walk to stretch my legs."

We buy some cold beer in a liquor store and head back to the little city park where migrant Latino families watch their children play tag and swing. Gene pours some of the Coors' Lite into my travel mug and I tell him again about these crazy feelings of abandonment. The wide open flat land we have driven through makes me notice the gnawing emptiness I feel inside. Gene's listening ears and watchful eyes look for ways to reassure me. "It's okay, kid. You've got good reason to cry. Roy's sudden death shook us all up. But you're gonna make it. I promise."

Early Sunday morning
The level land of Kansas, its elevation slanting upward towards the Colorado border, rolls up behind us as the map of New Mexico unfolds on my lap. "Where's Capulin and what is it?"

"Capulin is an extinct volcano in northeast New Mexico," he answers. "It's a national monument."

From a lookout on the drive up 818 ft. to the rim we survey the landscape. We seek and find a section of the old Santa Fe Trail. Deep ruts cut by iron wagon wheels leave evidence of a challenging journey across this empty space. We speak of families trudging through heat and cold, mud and snow, leaving footprints followed by thousands, all seeking their future or fortune. We try to imagine the courage it took to leave everything and carve a new trail to the unknown.

The need for endurance is magnified by a wide expanse of rangeland valley marked with mesas and volcanic hills. The majestic, snow-capped Sangre de Cristo Mountains break the horizon westward. I think my fears might reflect the fears of those earlier sojourners and icy fingers of self-doubt run down my spine. Shivering in the mid-morning sun I head back to the truck and see, what I sense to be, Roy's presence in the form of two, very different Monarch-sized butterflies. Their flashy bold colors of red and blue trimmed in black and white flair like the skirts of Spanish dancers as they fly over and around us turning me round and round to watch.

At the rim of Capulin, Gene starts a daily ritual of making me hike to some new place. His committed insistence will help me find my own way to living with mystery. For now we follow the 0.2 mile path down to the vent.

After lunch in Raton, New Mexico, Gene gives me the keys to his '99 Ford Ranger. He trusts me even if it is my first time to drive a pickup truck.

A few miles down the road seven or eight antelope, down from the dry brown hills and looking for a little green grass, run across the road in front of the truck. I'm distracted. Gene is pointing out the National Rifle Association headquarters hunkered low and back from the road. The antelope are fast enough to save us and the truck from disaster.

At Ghost Ranch, Abiquiu, New Mexico
This could be a healing place. There is space for the depth and breadth of my emotions. Dry earth yearns to soak up my tears. The canyon walls open wide but the echo of my sobs pull me close to what feels like the bosom of Mother Earth. Hope stretches beyond my reach to the horizon. Everything seems sacred. I have come into the sanctuary of God.

I find the writing class lays out the tools we can use to tell our stories and find our voice. The poet emerging from within mystifies Gene. I don't know what to think.

Afternoons we hike – up Box Canyon to the graves of saints, along the windy Chama River where we stumble over long abandoned adobe ruins, behind Staff House across the dry creek bed and up and around an unidentified mound.

Friday evening – the return from Abiquiu Inn after dinner with classmates
We round a curve at the top of the desert and catch a glimpse of a sunset painted by the closing of day.

The colors of the artist's pallet are brushed across an expanse of canvas sky. Orange, pink, lavender from blue to purple. Ordinary words sound feeble as I attempt to describe the handiwork of God.

The setting of this New Mexico sun, its light fading into the velvet black of night, is like a symbol of the darkness of grief that has replaced the beautiful life I have just lost. The last glimmer of light is a pause between my past with Roy and my future without him.

Gene Blake reflects

For months Sherry and I had planned to go to Ghost Ranch. The year before I'd gone alone, made the trip home in one day, and it had taken me two weeks to recover. My health had made traveling alone a risky venture. We were blessed because Roy and my wife, Mary, trusted us to travel together. Sherry had not planned to take the writing class for which I'd signed up. However, her class was cancelled because of limited applicants, and she was placed in her second choice, Creative Non-fiction.

Then Roy died. That Saturday night Mary and I immediately drove to Wichita when we heard the news. I knew from my experience leading a bereavement support group Sherry would suffer shock because of his unexpected death, and the reorientation of her life would be a difficult challenge.

But what about the trip to Ghost Ranch? Should she go? Would she go? The decision had to be hers, and I didn't believe it was wise for me to offer negative or positive suggestions. Providing a supportive presence seemed to be the best alternative.

I knew leaving her home and traveling to Ghost Ranch would be a time of tears and talk. So was the week of writing about her loss and grief. Yet it had its healing effect. Writing, like talking, helps us work through the grieving process and maintain a healthy perspective. Some of the pieces she wrote that week appear in this book.

The writing class that year was small and provided a warm and accepting environment. Our instructor, Ina Hughs, couldn't have been more sensitive and compassionate. The beauty of the desert landscape was a source of inspiration and awe. A sunset, far exceeding all others I've experienced, added to the magic of the time. In retrospect, Sherry's decision to make the trip was a wise one. She met the challenge of facing her loss as she talked and wrote about the experience. She plumbed the depths of her emotions and learned to put them into words.

Life Together

> *"If we make our goal to live a life of compassion and love,*
> *then the world will indeed become a garden*
> *where all kinds of flowers can blossom and grow."*
> Calligraphy by Elinor Holland

Falling in love with you
like bowling a 300 game and keeping the score sheet.
Being in love with you
like adding chapters to a Gothic novel.
Loving you
is satisfying like beef burritos and frozen margaritas.

    God is good – these are the ways
Meeting you at Deluxe Bowl on North Washington Street in Wichita.
Calling you "Babe." Signing my notes, "Love, Me!"
Roy says, "Say good night, dear." I say, "Good night dear!" and we laugh.

    God is good – these are the ways
Tailgate parties with hot dogs in a thermos,
Walks around the block in the dark,
Picnics in the park with wine in real glasses,
Applauding your successes at banquets.

    God is good – these are the ways
No talking to you before breakfast,
My reading the newspaper last,
Clean socks and shorts in your drawer,
Running the sweeper for me and doing the wash when I was away.

    God is good – these are the ways
Remembering you liked apple pie not cherry,
Ketchup but not tomatoes.
My eating sardines only when you were out of town.
Popcorn with extra butter and salt for me at the movies.

God is good – these are the ways
Dinner ready and waiting for you when we were young,
Cooking together when we were older – I talked; you chopped.
Your hot Gun Powder Dip, homemade dipped chocolates
and cinnamon suckers,
Eating cornbread, ham 'n beans with white Karo syrup and ketchup.

God is good – these are the ways
My commitment to seek justice and peace,
Your quiet mentoring of others,
Our stewardship of life and things,
Our love of children and support for the rights of women and minorities.

God is good – these are the ways
Buzzing Grandma Brown's Terrace Gardens Apartment in a Cessna 152,
Taking pictures while flying low over Grandma and Granddad Phillips' farm
at Emporia.
Flying me to speak in churches in small towns all over Kansas and Missouri;
Flying to Texas and California for weddings.

God is good – these are the ways
Watching Wichita State University Shocker Basketball games;
You cheered and kept score; I cheered and read a book.
Hosting Shocker baseball watch parties from the Cessna Skybox;
Me fixing coffee and reading; you watching outside in the cold while listening
to the game with Mike Kennedy's play-by-play on radio plugged into your ear.

God is good – these are the ways
Practicing for retirement,
With trips to Hawaii, the Smokey Mountains, Lafayette, and Mobile,
Planning for our 40th wedding anniversary – a 2003 trip to the Netherlands
that would include a visit to Cessna's branch office.

God is good – these are the ways
Exchanging smiles and blown kisses across the TV room,
Candles and cards,
Yellow roses on June 15th
Anniversary movie dates

God is good – these are the ways.
Learning to be intimate together,
Sex in the early morning light –
The difference between sparklers and the annual 4th of July Extravaganza at Cessna Stadium.
Your back rubs and back scratches,
My soft pats on your shoulders,
Holding hands under the covers while drifting off to sleep.

God is good – these are the ways
Drinking Blue frozen Raspberry Bellinies for lunch in Alabama,
Pork tip burritos and strawberry margaritas at the Cactus on Friday nights,
Diet Rite cola from a "jug."

God is good – these are the ways
Birthing two sons – Shane in 1963 and Jason in 1969.
T-ball and soccer; broken bones and stitches.
Graduations from WSU – you, then Shane, then Jason and Kristen.

God is good – these are the ways
Shane and Shelley marrying in Irving, Texas,
Jason and Kristen's wedding at Blessed Sacrament.
Enjoying responsibility and independence – ours and theirs,
Celebrating growing families with card games and dominoes.
Crock pots full of gun powder dip; celery stuffed with sardine stuff.
Grandchildren numbering four
Foot massages, group hugs, phone calls: "Hi, Mimi! Where's Papa? Love you! "Bye!"

God is good – these are the ways
Living the stories of our life with almost 39 chapters together,
Holding you as you died on March 23rd
Celebrating your life with a cloud of 500 witnesses –
family, Cessna Aircraft co-workers, friends, and neighbors.
Remembering!

God is good! These are only a few of the ways.

Butterfly

I wrote this May 6, 2002, in the Creative Writing course at Ghost Ranch in New Mexico. The assignment was to write an analogy using a diagram of something with its different parts named.

"Before I was dead, but now I am alive," says the butterfly, the ancient symbol for Christians of their Savior's resurrection. The smallest of children can accept the mystical scenario of Caterpillar spun into Chrysalis and emerged winged creature that rewards all patient observers.

Even Christians who probe the mysteries of science find easy evidence of the three in one in this most beautiful of species. Caterpillar, Chrysalis, and Butterfly share an abdominal segment. Simple eyes in the Caterpillar multiply to compound for the Butterfly while Chrysalis is not using them. Chrysalis and Butterfly share the required antenna needed to orient and locate.

Chrysalis cannot say I have no need for the walking leg of a Caterpillar or the hind, middle and forelegs of Butterfly and Butterfly cannot say I have no need for the cremaster that attaches Chrysalis to hang from twig or limb. Without walking legs Caterpillar could not get to twig or limb. Without hind, middle and forelegs Butterfly could not prepare for the safe place for Caterpillar to begin the next journey. Without a cremaster Chrysalis could not form the tomb of transformation for Butterfly.

Three in one. We can say that Chrysalis creates, Butterfly saves, and Caterpillar sustains. For Christians, Jesus Christ, the long-expected Savior, is God, and the Holy Spirit, the sustaining presence of God, gifted to humankind for their faith journey through life. The journey each one travels from first breath until last is not traveled alone.

We being many are one. White cannot say to brown I have no need of you. And black cannot say to red I have no need of you. North cannot cut off the South. East inevitably meets west. Food buyers need farmers. Tax collectors are useless without taxpayers. Have-nots define haves. Life needs oxygen, oxygen is a by-product of green plants and trees; greenery requires water, and water collects in the oceans and lakes then evaporates. Icebergs slip into the sea. Warm and cold air currents collide to produce storms heavy with moisture that rains or snows down on every continent. Life cannot say, "I have no need for water."

As a Christian, I use the vocabulary of this concept of three in one. But how life begins, life itself, and how life ends are the myths and stories woven into the fabric of beliefs of every tribe and nation. The temptation to describe the indescribable, to define the indefinable, to believe the unbelievable challenges all who gather into their community. The inevitable necessity of describing, defining, and believing requires a truth that separates, excludes, and insists.

How can there be three in one? How can one include all? There is no question if humankind could but enjoy the beauty of Butterfly, experience the unfolding mystery of Chrysalis, and give thanks for life lived as Caterpillar. Do you not see? Have you not heard?

Gene Blake reflects

When life is easy and carefree we seldom struggle with its great questions ... questions like:
- How did humanity come into being?
- How can every person be a unique creation?
- Is there life beyond death?
- Is there a God and, if so, what role does God play in our lives?

But in the face of death we can be overwhelmed by these questions. We seek answers where before we didn't even have questions. I maintain everyone has a theology – a perspective on life from which they establish values and priorities. Granted, many theologies are not very enlightened. As a pastor I've seen some unusual theologies present themselves when the bereaved try to make sense of their situation.

However, a discussion of theology with a grief stricken person is usually unwise. Arguing theology at this time can be downright insensitive – possibly even cruel.

It is a wise person, like Sherry, who has struggled with the great questions of life and death long before being faced with the loss of a loved one. Faith can be a great source of comfort, but the doctrinal aspects of faith seldom provide that comfort. I'm reminded of a comment by a friend and Roman Catholic sister, Mary Jo Ritter: "When it comes to matters of doctrine and dogma, I have a difficult time getting past the belief that God is love." But many of us find it all too easy to get past that point and, in an unloving fashion, expound upon our questionable beliefs. It is God's love, expressed through the actions of loving friends and family, that the bereaved find most comforting – not a discussion of the arcane points of theology. Human beings are a highly interdependent species and at no time is this more evident than during the grieving process.

Wise persons realize they do not have to have answers to all their questions and are content to live with mystery. It's very human to want certainty in life, but faith, by definition, is not certainty. Who are we to think we can fully define God or to question the nature of life on earth? ✤

I Am Sorry for Your Loss

"Whoever conceals grief finds no remedy for it."
Turkish Proverb

I tell my grandkids things we lose fall into a big black hole. But keep hoping. Maybe the hole will cough back up what's lost. It happens. A sock goes into the washer and never comes out of the dryer. Black hole got it. Now and then, an extra sock comes out of the dryer, but we've already thrown away its mate. Just in case, a look in the rag bag is the expression of hope a pair can be restored. I do believe the black hole can even cough twice. What's lost is often found.

I try to convince myself that Roy is in Phoenix on Cessna business or somewhere in Europe working to certify the latest Cessna Citation jet he's been working on. Roy is not lost if I know where he is.

Yet here is a stack of cards full of words of condolence. Dozens more arrive each day. They pile up here on the table, acidic reminders that Roy is not lost. He is not traveling on business. Shock after his death has slipped into the darkness leaving me in the stark daylight of reality.

"Sorry for your loss," the cards say. Flowery phrases, some nakedly brief, others with so many unreadable, unbelievable words reminding me of Roy's absence. The black hole that engulfs Roy is not going to release him. He is buried in the ground. He is dead.

A Contemporary Psalm of Lament

"When I despair, I remember that all through history the way of truth and love has always won ... Think of it, always."
Mahatma Gandhi

O Lord, come close and cradle me in my bereavement,
My beloved has died and half my heart ripped away.
I am afraid of waking in the middle of the night,
The valley next to me no longer holds the love of my life.
My breathing is accompanied by silence.
An empty room hears me crying.
The darkness of dreams vanished keeps me from remembering.
I am alone in the light and in the night.
I am overwhelmed by all of the things that must be done,
My partner for discernment can no longer speak.
Our plans for two have been crumpled like paper in the powerful hands of
"Death too soon."
No workshop, conference, or meeting has prepared me to go into
the future alone.
Husband, lover, partner, companion, and friend are gone.
Electrician, plumber, carpenter, lawn, and handyman are no more.
In the absence of father, son, brother, uncle, neighbor, and Papa,
My ripped apart heart must love double.
More of me is needed but only half of me exists.

But, You, O God, have always been faithful and our strength in times of death, Your presence brightens the darkened hall.
Your light beckons me to continue to put one foot in front of the other.
You nudge me and enable me to see people and places as loving reminders that my hurting heart still beats.
You strengthen me with sweet reminders of Roy's presence. Blessings appear when sought and arrive as unexpected gifts.
The beauty of butterfly, the coo of mourning dove, the hum of a single engine Cessna.
His favorite Cherry Mash candy bar at the bottom of a "welcome to St. Joseph, MO" bag.
ROY 545 and RRP 212 – car tags quietly affirming his existence.
The envelope addressed by his hand and containing a paper describing his goals for the coming year, folded carefully and arriving by mail months after we kissed him good-by.
Therefore, O God, give me courage to wait in the darkness of an empty and hurting heart,
Give me the comfort of Your tender embrace.
Let my head rest on Your strength while tears overflow eyes that no longer see visions and dream dreams.
Give me patience and courage to live through this sudden, overwhelming loss.
Grant me strength to face the difficulties that accompany a walk with grief.
Unstop my ears that I might hear the words of assurance that come from those who care.
Open my eyes to see the face of Christ in the face of others.
Let me feel Your tender care as they hold me like a fragile bone China tea cup in the palms of their hands.
Keep the presence of my beloved Roy just a breath away.
And when the time comes, give me courage to sing a new song and to dance.
You have created and saved the world.
We trust in the meaning You give to life even as we trust in its mystery.
By the love of Christ our Savior You mend broken hearts and fill the emptiness.
O, Lord, I will keep on loving You till the end of my days.
I will let my love for Roy heal my open and wounded heart.
Be now my Comforter and Hope. Amen.

Rude Awakening to Anger

"Anger is the external expression of inward hurt."
Rebecca New, *Presbyterian Clergywoman*

In a Wizard of Id cartoon in the *Wichita Eagle*, two scarf and apron festooned women leave the cemetery – one all broken up and weeping. The other looking perplexed says, "The only thing wrong with Earl is that he never put the toilet seat down."

Roy always put down the seat and lid. Lucky me. For some reason I always thought it was important.

What did tick me off was the way he clipped his toe nails. Oh, he cut them just the way a podiatrist says to do it – straight across. It was the way he would drag the sharp, pointed corner of his big toe nail across the bottom of my feet under the covers at night. What a rude awakening. I would just give him a swift little kick. Then I realized he was just stretching his legs before rolling over. Not really anything to get mad about.

Maybe a bigger complaint was about Roy's handwriting. The only place it really mattered was in the checkbook. Roy was the bill payer-investor-bank statement reconciler-paper pusher half of our partnership. He was efficient, neat and tidy. Kept records and reports current. Even made inventories of our U.S. Savings Bonds and had a list of contents of our safe deposit box in his computer.

But I almost needed a Navaho code breaker for his shorthand in the checkbook. The first three entries were the same each month. I just could not figure out his notations. I couldn't tell where the money went. The postings were of automatic debits so I ended up going to the bank for information. I was frustrated.

"Do I hear a hint of anger?" It was a good question. Burning tears of embarrassment flowed in streams down my checks. Overwhelmed with things to do and unable to complete even the simplest of tasks I could not understand the value of my friend's question – at first.

Mad at Roy? No! It was the damn handwriting. How could I be mad at Roy? I can't even be mad at God. Roy didn't die to hurt me. Hell, the doctor said Roy wouldn't have even known he was dying when he fell to the ground. If I had just stayed home – not gone shopping or gotten home earlier. Mad at Roy? How could I be?

❦
Gene Blake reflects

The most important lesson in life is learning to live with imperfection – our imperfection and that of others. Marriage is a classic example. The perfect spouse does not exist – not even in death.

Yet it's difficult to be objective about a loved one following their demise. The temptation is to gloss over their imperfections and make them just a little larger than life. At other times we may rail against the fact we must learn how to perform the tasks the deceased assumed as part of the typical division of labor existing in most marriages. It's advisable to learn to balance the checkbook before our bookkeeper mate dies.

Some may question my premise about learning to live with imperfection. But it's quite basic. Why does an infant cry so much? The baby is learning to live with imperfection now that they're out of the perfect environment of the womb. They have to endure hunger, noise, dirty diapers, even temporary separation from a parent. It takes them decades to learn to live with imperfect parents. Then they have to learn to live with their own imperfect children. Living with imperfection is a basic, universal challenge for all people.

Lives there a person who has not been critical of their spouse? Only a select few fully appreciate the fine qualities of a husband, wife, or child while overlooking their shortcomings.

I've found it fascinating how we're so inclined to praise someone at their funeral, but would never compliment them about those same qualities while they were alive. And it's remarkable how a pastor can gloss over some obvious shortcomings: a person was persistent, not stubborn, had an earthy sense of humor rather than told dirty stories and was a person of principle, not argumentative. The minister who officiated at my father's funeral praised him so much I was tempted to check the casket. And while doing a eulogy for a good friend who was a farmer/rancher and local leader, I found myself mentioning all the ways he served his community but, to add some authenticity to my comments, I noted, "The only thing I ever found to criticize about Duane was the fact he didn't fix fence any better than my dad."

Many deceased spouses probably would be surprised to find they've become "sudden saints" – far more admired in death than in life. The same thing happened to Abraham Lincoln and John Kennedy. Time, however, adds objectivity … and turns saints back into the imperfect human beings they were before they died – whether they're presidents or just folks. 🍁

Hugging Helps

"We always close our evenings together with a hug. Hugging helps." Beth then proceeded to give each of the Good Grief Support Group participants a hug. And like ants following their leader we turned to one another and hugged our way around the circle making sure we left no one out.

Alone. The empty chair, the untouched toothbrush, one fork, one knife, one spoon in the dishwasher, no dress shirts to pick up at the laundry, no undershirts or shorts in the dirty clothes hamper. All reminders that Roy, my husband and lover of almost 39 years, was never, ever coming back.

He was not in Phoenix or in Europe or visiting our kids in Texas. He was gone, passed away, with Jesus in heaven. The awful fact was that he was just plain dead. His familiar body was lying cold in a grave at Lakeview Cemetery.

As Roy lay silent in the casket ready for our last look and prayer before the funeral, I can still hear Rev. Dennis say, "Remember, Sherry, Roy isn't here. This is only his body, an empty vessel." My murmured response was, "Yes, but it is his body that I could hold."

I can only now describe what I must have meant then. No more hugs and kisses to give and to get. No more cold feet and warm body next to mine in our queen size bed. No more quiet snoring to awaken me for an opportunity for middle of the night lovemaking. No more hand holding under the covers or on a walk around the block. No more winks and silent sent kisses from his chair across the TV room. No sounds of early morning bathroom chores to be followed by a quick 6 a.m. sexual encounter made all the more fun because the sons were gone from home making families of their own.

Beth was right. Hugging helps. To touch another and to be touched by someone who knows the same awful loneliness you do brings comfort. Someone stepping into personal space with the intent to express, "I understand" with hugs and soft pats on the shoulder offers a life link. Hugs give strength and courage to one another to keep going along the grief journey. A reminder we don't travel alone. Mutual assurance that we can make it through to define our new life.

It helps until someone holds me too tight and too long. Hugs help unless they are expressed in a full frontal press. When a guy in the group steps into my personal space to talk about how alone he feels, a yellow caution flag waves in my mind. Hands touching my cheeks or placed on my knee are unwanted. Fingers on the back of my neck and hands massaging my shoulders were Roy's intimate touches. Hugs help but eyes that look for an opportunity to invite a get together so "we won't be so alone" suggest too much. A suggestion I have no need for now.

To be truthful, in the first few weeks after Roy died, I longed for our pattern of sexual encounters. Even now I dream of having sex with him. I write about these feelings because I can now identify what it is I really miss.

What I miss most is just his presence. Laying back-to-back on a cold night. His middle to put my arm around. His bare shoulders to stroke. His arms around me pulling me tight and pressing his body tight next to mine. My hand held in his under the covers as his lips whisper, "'night Babe."

I miss these sustaining intimacies. I want my partner back. But I know that is not possible. I also know that until my heart feels healed, until I have made a successful adjustment to my aloneness there can be no room in my bed for another. Or, maybe never.

Gene Blake reflects

Years ago, when I was leading support groups for people who were widowed and divorced, a woman coined a new term to describe our basic desire for physical contact with another human being. "Skin hunger" she called it. Everyone in the group seemed to understand what she meant.

Beginning at birth we have a yearning to be held – pressed tightly against our mother's breast, encircled, warmed, comforted, consoled, and made to feel secure. Because babies fail to thrive when they aren't held, one can make the case that physical contact is a need, not just a want – a need that extends even into adulthood. With sexual maturity the desire for physical contact takes on a broader context. Granted the sex drive is necessary for the procreation of our species, but sexual expression also involves intimacy, love, companionship, communication, pleasure, etc.

As intelligent human beings we try very hard to be rational and reasonable. We create cultures and social structures to regulate our relationships with others. But our sexuality often pays little attention to social norms. In some ways it's animal-like, yet it has the capability to far transcend the sexual expression of animals. Sexuality involves our emotions and senses – sight, smell, hearing, and, most significantly, touch. Although the brain is the primary sex organ, its intellectual side only exerts partial control over our emotions and expressions. The powerful and prideful often find themselves humbled by their sexuality. The wise are awed by this intricate aspect of our humanity.

An ancient author, writing a story of creation, made the observation, "It is not good for man to be alone." When the man was presented with the presence of a woman, he exclaimed, "This is now bone of my bones, flesh of my flesh!" The writer concluded, "For this reason a man will leave his father and mother and be united to his wife, and they will become one."

This passage is often used as a scripture reading at weddings. But one could make the case for it being more appropriate at funerals – at least this was the consensus of the bereavement support group I led. The recently bereaved often feel as if they have lost half of themselves. Some even experience physical pain. Ancient wisdom is correct: "The two have become one." Losing a spouse is like losing a part of ourselves – our identity, our companion, our lover, our future together. "Skin hunger" is a symptom of this loss.

We are relational human beings. We desire intimacy – intimacy in all its ramifications:
- Intellectual intimacy. Sharing ideas, viewpoints.
- Emotional intimacy. Sharing our feelings of love, anger, fear, worry, joy. Being close enough to cry together.
- Spiritual intimacy. Sharing similar values, priorities, and faith expressions. Being "soul mates."
- Physical intimacy. Sharing kisses and caresses, sharing our bodies in a bond of love, satisfying our "skin hunger," and becoming "one flesh."

Usually the quality of a couple's sexual relationship is proportional to the presence of intellectual, emotional, and spiritual intimacy. We have that innate desire "to become one."

"It's not good for man to be alone" – it's not good for women either. When we find ourselves suddenly single we feel vulnerable, insecure, inadequate, not sure of ourselves. Marriage usually gives us a feeling of wholeness. Widowhood makes us feel broken. I've confessed to the divorced and bereavement support groups I've led, "If I were to find myself divorced or widowed I'd probably do something truly stupid out of loneliness!" Even that self-knowledge would probably not preclude my making some unwise choices and decisions. "Skin hunger" is a powerful desire. When we're widowed it is one of the most basic, yet least discussed, aspects of being newly alone. ✤

The Significance of Sexual Love

A three-minute in-class writing assignment at Ghost Ranch was destined to be in this book.

Sexual love is only one part of the banquet of partnerships.
For some it is the main course, the entrée.
But in my experience it was dessert.
A satisfying reward for working our way through a seven-course meal served with elegance over our 40 years together.

Dust

"My strength is gone, gone like water spilled on the ground. All of my bones are out of joint; my heart is like melted wax. My throat is as dry as dust and my tongue is as dry as dust ... you have left me for dead in the dust."
Psalms 22:11-15

"Ashes to ashes and dust to dust." These words from the committal service at Lakeview Cemetery months ago are beginning to wander through my mind. They remind me of the dry, warm, breezy wind kicking up dry grass and the winter dust that swirled around shocked and disbelieving mourners, clutched and waiting for the final amen.

What is this dust stuff? I can never figure out a good reason for it. Roy is dead. Decay should disappear instead of turning into a fine, talc-like residue that finds a way to layer itself on everything that lies still for too long.

Men do not worry about dust. I question why God didn't consult a woman before designing this part of the mystery of life.

But dust is! And it aptly describes the musty, choky feeling I have as I try to sort through memories stored over the years in the basement closet of my mind. Those words and their wanderings stir up stuff layering the fading experiences of forty years. These snapshots lay scattered about instead of neatly sorted and filed by event, names, ages, or dates.

In June and early August my two computer-savvy sons took turns "de-fragging" the hard drive on my laptop. They described the task to me like this. The computer stores what I tell it to save in the closest convenient place on the hard drive and that wastes space in its memory.

They didn't use this example but my hard drive must look like my office desk, dining room table, buffet, and chairs on any given day of the week. My latest project gets set down on any flat place when the phone rings, mail comes, cards need to be written, lunch eaten, or bills paid. I do an occasional cleaning and restack the accumulation from time to time. I even file things in places that should make sense.

Shane and Jason tell me this "de-fragging" makes room in the memory and can speed up my computer. There are advantages to having an efficient retrieval system.

However, God did not incorporate a de-fragging program into human hard drives. Designed without the advice of computer genius our minds have no choice but to store memories in dusty, musty places wherever space can be found.

This is my mind today. Five months ago Roy died too young, without warning, of cardiac arrhythmia. I am wandering in this musty basement closet sifting through memories, half-forgotten or remembered in bits and pieces. My eyes sting and blur with tears. Almost 40 year's accumulation of memories catches in my throat like dust:
—the Deluxe Bowling Alley where we met and that Roy managed at night while working his way through the first two years of college
—an ROTC dance at the Cotillion Ballroom wearing his Air Force blue uniform and me in a borrowed strapless blue taffeta trimmed in black lace
—Christmas Eve draw name gift exchanges with food and cards at his folks' house
—the yellow wedding roses and glorious flower bouquets celebrating anniversaries
—picnics in the park and football tail gate parties

—Thanksgiving dinners shared with my family with Roy cooking the turkey
—Shane, our first-born son and fifth generation Phillips' boy pictured with great-grandpa Phillips, grandpa Ray, and his Daddy, Roy
—second-born son, Jason, in his orange pajamas sitting on grandma Ruth's lap and holding his orange and brown teddy bear made by great-grandma Phillips
—those first days of preschool and kindergarten and graduations from East High School and Wichita State University
—Six Flags over Texas, Disney World, Mount Rushmore, and Silver Dollar City
—the '56 green and white Chevy, '59 tomato-red Chevrolet Impala two-door with stick shift and a 283 V-8 engine, a blue-green and white Chevy II with extra gas tank in the trunk, the hatch-back green Gremlin, plain gray Chevette, navy blue Volkswagen Golf, and the '93 plus '92 teal blue Saturns
—all those home remodels on South Estelle
—albums of grandchildren, Derek and Abby down Highway I-35 to Texas and Krystine and Hannah on Clark Street only eight blocks away.

The file folders have names but the memories are scattered about and all mixed together. Oh God, defragment this mind of mine. Let all of these bits and pieces return smiles to my face. Let the tears that spill from my eyes rinse away my sadness. Let the warmth of remembered embrace keep loneliness at bay.

Is this the reason for dust dear Lord? To remember what we only think has been forgotten? Could it be true, as the months come and go without the love of my life, nothing will disappear? Will there always be some special something to remind me of the jillions of little things that made our life together a family?

If dust and ashes can stir up memories, surely hope is possible. God must have consulted a grieving heart – the very own heart of God – to have such a good reason to create dust.

Gene Blake reflects

The committal statement I've used hundreds of times at untold cemeteries concludes: "...earth to earth, ashes to ashes, dust to dust. Blessed are the dead who die in the Lord, says the Spirit. They rest from their labors, and their works follow them." That last phrase, "...their works follow them," certainly applies to Roy.

During the service, he was praised by a retired Cessna vice-president who was once Roy's supervisor. Roy had a reputation of mentoring and grooming rather than aspiring to a position of personal power and prestige. He was on a first-name basis with people who worked in all areas of the plant. Because he had worked his way up from loading dock to the front office, he had earned their respect.

Not only did Roy graduate from WSU, he continued to support the institution. Professionally, he worked with the engineering departments of WSU and other state universities to help them better prepare their students. Personally, he attended most Shocker baseball and basketball games – supporting them with his presence and money. His works follow him. Roy sang in the choir of Mt. Vernon Presbyterian Church and had served on its governing body. Church attendance was a regular event for him. No one would call him a "C and E" (Christmas and Easter) Christian.

Roy was dependable. Effusive and flamboyant are not the words one would choose to describe him. Humble, pragmatic, stalwart, and consistent are far more appropriate. He served as a role model by the material choices he made.

Is Roy Phillips' memory just dust? Hardly. But it seems to me that he, like many of our loved ones, was more appreciated in death than in life.

Practically everyone has positive traits and accomplishments we should value as we reflect on their life. Following Roy's death, Sherry feared she and others would forget about him. I'm not sure if this is a common fear, but I would encourage the bereaved to talk about the deceased. Sharing stories and valuing their memory can insure that "their works will follow them."

Is That You Babe?

> *"Believing is not about truth. It is about presence.*
> *God meeting a need at special times in our lives. It is incarnation."*
> Rev. Tom Oak, *Presbyterian Pastor*

No matter what anyone says I know it was Roy. A shuffling sound woke me in the dark of early morning. "What? What's wrong?" my voice sounding sleepy to my ears. "Don't worry, I'm just looking for my comb," was the familiar reassurance.

Sometimes it was his badge or his favorite pen. His dresser drawer would open or the closet door followed by searching sounds – rifling through the pockets of pants or suit coat worn the day before. Necessities are hard to find in the dark. Leaning up on one elbow, squinting into the dark I knew there was no one to see this time.

My hesitant sharing of this early morning encounter with the circle of grief group members was like a head nod for Helen to share about seeing Bert standing at the end of their bed. Then Marian told us about the soft pull on her toes just like the routine way Jesse had awakened her each morning when he returned from early morning coffee with his buddies.

The recording of *To Where You Are* by Josh Groban was already a favorite of mine before Roy died. The words have real meaning now.

"Who can say for certain?
Maybe you're still here.
I feel you all around me, your memories so clear.
Deep within the stillness I can hear you speak.
You're still an inspiration.
Can it be that you are my forever love,
and you are watching over me from up above?
Fly me up to where you are beyond the distant star
I wish upon tonight to see you smile, if only for awhile
to know you're there. A breath a way's not far too where you are.
Are you gently sleeping here inside my dream?

And isn't faith believing all power can't be seen?
As my heart holds you just one beat away, I cherish all you gave me every day.
'Cause you are my forever love watching me from up above.
And I believe that angels breathe and that love will live on and never leave.
Fly me up to where you are beyond the distant star
I wish upon tonight to see you smile, if only for awhile to know you're there.
A breath away's not far to where you are. I know you're there."

Excuses For Not Writing

"Procrastination is a form of resistance to our personal growth and healing."
Joe Stumpe, Reporter for *The Wichita Eagle*

Writing something creative is hard.
I forget to write.
At 7:30 a.m. I need coffee and a powdered sugar donut from Chicago Donuts.
I sit at the counter, fourth stool left of the showcase.
Yogi asks me how I am and means it.
I read the daily Wichita Eagle with my second cup of coffee.
I begin to worry about what's going wrong with the world.
Work the crossword puzzle and Jumble before Chief comes in for his coffee and maple long john. He sits in his truck to get a head start.
Computer is at home.
The computer refuses to boot up when I get home.
Computer boots up; I check for e-mail messages on AOL
before computer shuts itself off.
AOL connects when it gets around to it.
E-mail is answered.
Snail mail comes.
Phone rings. Looks like another telemarketer.
Coffee break – instant decaf heated in the microwave.
I start a small load of laundry.

Put newspapers in recycle bin for pick up.
Sit down again at the computer.
Computer refuses to boot up, again.
I try again.
Software scans the drive because it detected an improper shut down.
Why does it blame me?
Don't know what to write.
I consider lunch.
I fix cheese with crackers; apple and milk. I should eat more veggies.
Afternoon break. I nuke, again, the last cup of instant I find left in the microwave.
Put wet clothes in dryer.
Phone call from a telemarketer – I decide to pick up.
Time to leave for Grief Group.
Dinner at Mickey D's first. I have my regular McChicken sandwich, dollar fries and large diet coke with extra of ice.
I dine in.
I puzzle, again, over the morning crossword clues that give me no clue.
Guilt. When I get home I should file or fold clothes.
Guilt. I ought to pay bills.
Guilt. I could run the sweeper, clean the bathrooms or wash dishes.
Plain old guilt.
No energy.
Too much to do first.
Writing makes me cry.
My eyes are drawn to watch the henbit purple
and dandelion yellow of summer.
I take a walk around the block.
Can't concentrate.
I can't think of anything to write.
Guilt.

Gene Blake reflects

Writing is but one example of the tasks we find difficult to accomplish while in the midst of grieving. The loss of a loved one can adversely affect our self-discipline, organization, concentration, creativity. Our energy is sapped and with it our desire to complete the tasks at hand. It's hard to do the urgent, let alone the important. The more challenging the task, the less we're inclined to tackle it. Even what used to be routine is now difficult. We accuse ourselves of being lazy and then feel guilty about it.

Our life seems to be on a treadmill of grief. We're going nowhere. All around us are unwanted responsibilities, and nowhere do we see any accomplishments. Working our way through grief is like entering a seemingly endless maze of tasks, frustrations, and lame excuses for not successfully finding an exit. We ask ourselves, "Where is this once competent person who used to be me?"

Take heart. That person is still there and will one day return. It won't be as soon as we like, but we will again find the energy and interest to be vital and capable. The computer will still be there; we will supply it with new ideas, new stories, and insights into life and death issues. And what's more, we probably will become more sensitive to the needs of others, more capable of listening, and better equipped to help others who struggle with grief.

This Is No Picnic

Several years ago I challenged my Sunday school class to look for projects to clean up the environment. I decided to clean up the parking lot of the open 24 hours Checkers Grocery Store at the corner of Pawnee and K-15 highway in southeast Wichita.

It was July. My plan was to start early before the black top got hot and before the parking lot was full.

The challenge was bigger than I had imagined. Two large black lawn bags later I had only cleaned half of the lot. I expected pop cans and cigarette butts but not dirty diapers and broken beer bottles. Plastic cups with lids and straws were sitting upright and half-full of whatever had been refreshment the day before. Smashed glass, nails, and sharp miscellaneous metal pieces threatened to slice open my plastic bag and left my fingers bloody and sore.

When I finished my sweep of the parking lot I sorted through the debris in the tall weeds in the public area around the perimeter. Four bags of mentionable and unmentionables later I was done and done in.

Dog-tired, dirty and pleased with myself. I knew someone in Checkers would come out to thank me in person or at least send me a letter of commendation. I never heard a mumblin' word.

Early the next day I hurried over to Checkers to look again at my energetic stewardship. Oh, my God. The parking lot looked as if I had not picked up one single piece of someone else's unwanted leftovers. More dirty work was ready and waiting.

As I shuffle through my business files, hunt for Monday's mail, wonder where I laid my car keys, rearrange the stack of unread magazines, contemplate which phone calls to return and then take yesterday's coffee cups from the breakfast table-computer desk to the kitchen, I remember that day in Checkers parking lot. It was a dirty, rewarding day. But the next morning was a real downer.

I think it would be great if someone else would come in and clean up my cluttered, dirty mess. I would thank them profusely and send a bouquet of roses.

Feelings of being overwhelmed smother me. Frustration makes me unable to make a dent in my to-do list. Where is my to-do list?

The grief support group leader tells us these feelings are normal. The journey to come to acceptance with the death of a loved one is hard, dirty work. And each morning the work has to be done again.

I am thankful for the support of others who know what I am going through. I am glad I am not crazy, that my feelings are normal. The leaders tell us we grieve because we have loved. I knew I loved Roy before he died but now I have the confusion, low or no energy, can't stay on task heart pain to prove it.

But if I listen I can hear Roy saying to me, "Babe, your car keys are right where you left them." And he is right. Here they are on the dining room table under yesterday's mail. Thanks, Babe!

※

Gene Blake reflects

Many years ago, in preparation for a bereavement support group meeting, I read an article that coined the term "grief work." Grief work. Our group had expressed grief in terms like loss, suffering, emotional pain, loneliness, and disorientation. But "work" had not been used to describe the process they were experiencing.

We went on to liken the loss of a loved one to having a big pile of sand dumped in the corner of our yard – a pile of sand that has to be moved to an opposite corner. The vision of moving a pile of sand helped us express our grief. Work; grief is work.

One's first reaction is to resent having the sand dumped in the yard. How dare this happen? Why did it happen to me? How will I deal with it? Nothing, other than reality, motivates us to begin this process.

Eventually, we accept the task of moving this enormous pile of sand, or, as we were thinking of it, grieving. Then we struggle with the question of how. Do we begin right away or do we put it off? Will we seek help or try to do it ourselves? How much can others really help? Ultimately, isn't it our task? How long will it take? Won't there always be a little sand left behind?

A few people dig in and try to move a pile of sand all at once. Some people try to do their grief work too quickly and fail to let time demonstrate its healing power. Encouraged by social pressure to "move on with their lives," they feel compelled to suppress or deny the grief that overwhelms them. But impatience and grief blend like oil and water. Those people who move a pile of sand too quickly may find themselves exhausted before the job is completed. In a similar fashion, those who try to hurry their healing may find a pile of grieving that never gets done.

On the other hand, there are some people, not many, who never do their grief work. Their lives are like a once nice home with an ugly pile of sand in the front yard.

Like someone moving a pile of sand several shovels full a day, most people tend to work through their grieving a little bit at a time – typically over one to two years. But several shovels full a day does not reduce the size of the sand pile quickly. Every morning it looks as large as the day before – progress is barely distinguishable. The grieving process becomes a daily grind. The term, grief work, begins to seem more appropriate.

As we move a pile of sand, we greatly appreciate the helpful friend who stops by with a shovel to share our task. When we're grieving, the good friend who is willing to listen and understand makes our task seem less onerous. We also find comfort in knowing there are others who face a pile of sand called grief, just as we do. They understand our fears, frustrations, and fatigue. We are not alone. Our feelings are natural. Slowly we come to realize the importance of patience and perseverance. Because we love we also are vulnerable to loss and grief. Yet to love and to be loved is worth that risk. ❀

Anniversaries

> *"What we once enjoyed and deeply loved we can never lose,*
> *for all that we love deeply becomes part of us."*
> Helen Keller

My sons and their wives would call this a half-anniversary – a celebration six months after the special event. At 3:45 a.m. this September 23, the word that awakens my mind is "remember."

Our early wedding anniversaries were modest affairs. Roy would tell me to be ready right after he got home from work. He would change clothes and off we would go. The formula was dinner and a movie.

Years and years ago we saw a re-release of *Gone with the Wind* at the old Uptown Theatre on East Douglas. With a ceiling like the night sky, twinkling stars and all, the Uptown was special. The starlit sky shining on Roman columns helped the Uptown evolve into the Crown Uptown dinner theatre of current day. Several more of our anniversaries through the years were celebrated at this local attempt to be "Broadway."

Another year we saw the futuristic film, *Soylent Green*. Charlton Hesston and Edward G. Robinson were the big names in a B movie that portrayed a gruesome plan to control an over-populated and out-resourced USA in the 21st Century. The message from this thought provoking show was the beginning of Roy's great concern for zero population growth and led to our financial support for Planned Parenthood.

His anniversary gift surprises were usually large, extra-postage-needed cards. Often humorous, often suggestive, these Hallmark messages spoke of passion and great love. They were always signed with only his "Love, Roy" signature written large and flamboyant. For a quiet man these were his infrequent attempts to be vivacious.

In those early years, the cards were often attached to a small box wrapped, no-bow, plain using a piece of leftover paper from the wrapping box stored in a back closet.

Card and wrapped surprise would be hidden in the glove compartment of the car. The little plain boxes often held beautiful, dangling earrings. One year I found two pair – black with red rhinestones and black with white rhinestones.

I chuckle now because Roy never even wanted me to get my ears pieced. He was so sure I would wear dangling earrings! Maybe dangles seemed a bit racy for this plain-Jane-introvert I thought he had married. I now believe it might have been his way of showing me I was special in his life – even desirable.

There were other surprises. Two hand-embroidered Japanese kimonos to complement our interest in oriental art and home décor and another year the see-through jumpsuit with fluffy pink trim ordered from a catalog. I look back and remember how embarrassed I was and thinking he wanted something very different from what he had.

When anniversary twenty-five rolled around, our two sons hosted an open house and we displayed the petite, white, lace-layered wedding dress I had worn as a slender, red-haired, twenty-year-old madly in love with a young, brown-eyed, night shift bowling alley manager working his way through college seeking an electrical engineering degree.

This resurrected wedding album recalls anniversary gifts for the years that followed. The earring gifts turned to roses – most often long stemmed and yellow. These were a remembrance of the flowers I carried on our wedding day. My quiet engineer, more romantic than I ever gave him credit for, would add one more rose each year to the order from Tillie's Flower Shop.

On our thirty-fifth, the bags were packed and I was ready to go. He hurried home from work and changed from his business suit. Then we rushed downtown for a weekend at the brand new Old Town Hotel. He had the third-floor suite reserved and as we came into this former warehouse-urban renewal project-turned luxury hotel we continued a journey that would last his lifetime. On the table was a huge golden vase overflowing with thirty-five yellow roses. I could tell by his smile that his secret plan, worked out with the concierge, had worked perfectly.

With this memory nudged, I recall we were rumbled awake at two a.m. with the loud bass beat of music playing down on the street outside of our window. We sat in the dark leaning on the windowsill watching with amusement the studs strut from fancy cars across the street to mingle with the coveys of sexy ladies. From our vantage point they looked very young and all alike. The girls wore similar styled cropped tops and low slung shorts or slacks. Each top was a different color so they could signal their individualism. The young crowd, sporting hairstyles and using mannerisms cloned from television sitcom stars, were all laughing and flirting on the street outside the American Club. They seemed a long, long way from our stage in life. We confessed we had no envy or regret. We were content.

I remember the trip to Disney World, just the two of us. I was in St. Louis to spend a few days at the General Assembly of the Presbyterian Church. Roy flew the Cessna 182 RG into a small airport landing right on time then taxied to the hangar where I stood waiting.

I felt like Ingrid Bergman in Casablanca. Roy was my Humphrey Bogart.

His planning was testimony to what life was like with an engineer who had worked his way from the warehouse, to the wiring shop, to a hoped-for tool and die training that turned into an offer to move right on into the engineering department at Cessna before his mechanical engineering degree was completed (changed from an electrical degree so he could graduate sooner.)

His hard work and excellent organizational mind along with a willingness to learn management skills took him almost to the top. His title when he died was Director of Integrated Systems and Design for Cessna Aircraft Company. He worked there over 35 years.

And what did I ever give this love of my life? Lots of words – I love yous and words of encouragement, cards with words to express my pride in his accomplishments and words to support him when times were tough. Words, words, words sometimes accompanying a can of whole cashews or a new sport shirt but often new handkerchiefs or underwear. I am a practical woman. These practical gestures seem foolish as I write and remember. But my gifts to him would need to be described by him to have any real meaning.

You see, this half-anniversary means it has been six months today since I found him dying in the backyard that he was so proud of and obliged to mow, trim, and water.

So what does one do to honor a loved one, a life-partner, six months after their life has been celebrated and the physical presence we've known so well cannot be embraced? I awake on this "half-anniversary" wanting to capture a few more memories that seem to come a bit more readily now that I can no longer pretend the nightmare was only a figment of my imagination.

I want to get the birdseed and sunflower seeds bottled up and the birdfeeder cleaned out so Roy's friends will come back this winter. Maybe then I can pull the weeds from the elderberry bushes that have grown unmolested since that March spring day trimming. Dare I risk a sip of wine in a real glass? I could pack a lunch or stop by Mickey D's for one of Roy's favorite Big Macs with a diet coke and then drive to the cemetery. Oh, yes, and I think I will stop by the flower shop to pick up a yellow rose.

Gene Blake reflects

"Who we are and what we believe is largely based upon stories." I first heard this observation from a seventh grader – one wise beyond his years. More than we realize, our identity is intertwined with stories from our grandparents and parents and memories of our own experiences.

As intelligent human beings we're created with the capacity to remember – an under-appreciated ability, I maintain. Blessed with both long-term and short-term memory, we're even able to sort out what to retain and what to forget. In our minds we store memories of family traditions and defining moments.

A few years ago I officiated at the committal service for Pauline "Jerry" Foltz. This 94-year-old woman was apparently something of a character that'd created many fond memories for her family and friends. At the graveside, her twelve grandchildren and others retold those stories – mostly humorous ones – mingling laughter with tears. I'm sure sharing these memories affirmed her influence on them and reinforced their family bonds.

Her committal service has now become a significant memory for me. It's a story I love to share. How could I forget noting she was buried with a cell phone because she was always talking to someone on the phone? Weeks later her son, Paul, humorously remarked, "There's one thing I regret about Mom's service. I should have taken a tire iron and put a few dents in her casket." When I asked why, he remarked, "She never did operate a vehicle without a dent in it!" I wish I'd had the opportunity to have known Jerry and been a part of her stories.

For several months thereafter, I reflected on the role of memories in our lives. For those who grieve the loss of a loved one, there is comfort, joy, and reward to be found in thinking back over decades of shared experiences – tears, laughter, companionship, and love. These are stories of how a couple met, fell in love, created a family, and overcame the challenges of life – stories of work, play, travel, and intimacy.

Much of life is involved in creating memories – stories to share at family gatherings and other poignant times when we're open to their significance. And no time is more poignant than when family and friends gather to pay their last respects at the funeral of someone dear. When someone dies, suddenly our recollections take on new meaning. The stories and memories have greater value. We may even have an irrational fear of forgetting the loved one and his or her role in our life.

Some time ago, Forrest Robinson (a retired United Methodist minister) and Michael Wilder (chair of the Performing Arts Division at Southwestern College), along with Michael's wife and daughter, presented a unique program at the college. Forrest would tell heartfelt stories of his World War II experiences interspersed with instrumental music by the Wilders. I thought, "If I were telling those tragic stories of war I'd need a musical interlude to regain my composure." Tom Brokaw, in his book, The Greatest Generation, observed the experiences and memories of the Great Depression and WWII were like a refiner's fire defining those who endured them. Traumatic experiences often make or break an individual. People like Forrest Robinson were obviously "made" by this period of history. His WWII stories are an integral part of who he was and is.

My father was a storyteller – a quality I didn't appreciate when I was young. I got tired of hearing how our name was changed from Blöchinger to Blake when an ancestor enlisted in the Union Army during the Civil War. However, family stories took on new meaning when I traveled to Miltenberg, Germany, the storybook Bavarian village from where my ancestors emigrated. I saw the actual building where the Blöchingers operated a butcher shop for centuries. Nearby was a three-story hotel built by Hans Anton Blöchinger in 1788. It's still in use and his initials remain on a plaque above the entrance.

I'm still haunted by the memory of putting my daughter to bed when she was young and having her plead, "Daddy, tell me a story." Unlike her grandfather, I hadn't taken the time to reflect on my memories – I hadn't created any family stories from my experiences. I was unable to respond to her basic human need.

But all of us – as parents and grandparents, family and friends – have the opportunity to cherish memories. It's our responsibility to value and nurture memories – to formulate stories from them for future generations – to tell and retell them as my father did. Stories take on new meaning when enriched with a sense of humor – maybe even with embellishment. Good stories are created when we don't take ourselves too seriously, and when we develop an appreciation for the absurd. Always remember the importance of stories, for they define the individuals who played a role within them.

When the limited energy of ill health and aging are taking their toll, I may jokingly remark, "I wish I would get Alzheimer's so I'd forget how hard I used to be able to work!" But one of the great tragedies of this debilitating disease is its theft of our memories. Victims no longer know who they are – or were – for a person's identity is intertwined with memory.

My fishing buddy, Bob Terrell, often remarks, "We need to go fishing often so when we can no longer fish we will be able to sit in our rocking chairs and reminisce" – telling stories that begin, "Remember when …"

Memories, however, are not created in the mundane – those days that fade into a fog of boredom. Memories are created when we step out of the ordinary and into the unusual – when we forget our fears and open ourselves to new experiences,
new friends,
new environments,
new challenges.
Memories become stories when we pay attention.
When we pay attention to the strange coincidences,
the significance of a particular moment,
the incongruous situations,
the beauty of nature,
the complexity of humanity,
the call of God,
the touch of the Spirit, and
the lives that enrich our own. ✻

Get Some Boots

"Every step of the journey is the journey."
Author Unknown

Suppose I say the words, "take a hike."

And suppose I remind you of how difficult that can be if you are not prepared, if your physical condition resembles a fluffy, white hotel-room bath towel smelling of Spring Breeze.

Of how you begin to breathe hard when you haul a basket of dirty underwear and jeans downstairs to the laundry room. And how twisting and turning to take clean and rinsed clothes from the washer to put in the dryer, then bending again to put dry load into the basket makes your back stiff and sore. And of how your once-in-a-while sweats happen in the middle of hot August nights and are eventually cooled by the vigorous flapping of your lavender, cotton nightgown.

And suppose I remind you that right now the idea of lifting a forty pound backpack onto your weak shoulders makes you want to drive your red Saturn L200 to Java Villa to sit for the rest of the afternoon nursing a large cup of Fair Trade coffee called Sumatra Goya. With the free refill you'd have time to work the *Wichita Eagle*'s daily comic page crossword puzzle, Jumble, and Crypto Quip.

In fact, taking a hike is the furthest thing from your mind. Not only do you need to be physically fit you have to get prepared. You need a map with the destination marked with a big X. By the time you gather your diabetic meds, enough food for calorie-burning sweat work and enough individually wrapped lifesavers or single boxes of 100% pure juice for emergencies plus a change of underwear and a couple of clean shirts your pack would exceed the legal weight limit allowed for checked luggage when boarding a plane.

You're not apt to take a good fresh air stroll on the walk path around Cessna Park let alone a hike in the mountains of New Mexico.

But nobody asked you. Remember how Roy's sudden death made you feel like you walked off a precipice, tumbling down a mountainside, ending up in a pile of rubble? You had to dig yourself out and pull yourself up in order to stumble on down life's road alone. This trek of mourning and grief has been more like a hike up a forty-degree gravel covered grade carrying everything you own.

You know this journey is one which challenges many men and women. When you describe your loss and struggle, fellow travelers in the Good Grief support group nod with silent affirmation. You know they know what you mean.

With the challenge of clearing a new path in unknown territory, some of the best advice you've had was to buy a good pair of hiking boots because Gene Blake was going to make you hike in the high places around Ghost Ranch in northern New Mexico. The fawn-colored suede, steel-toed ankle boots bought on special at a Wal-Mart Super Store and found in the Sports section proved to be worth far more than the $49.95 you charged to your VISA card.

Remember how those boots gave you traction on the rocky path down into the mouth of the extinct volcano named Capulin on that first trip away from home after Roy died?

Remember how they strengthened your weak ankles and legs as you climbed back to the rim?

You've made it this far with some good advice and the helping hands of family and friends. And those boots. Now keep on hiking.

Christmas Without Papa

The Week of Thanksgiving, 2002
As soon as Shane pulled into the driveway, Derek was the first out carrying Space Bee, a Teddy bear with his ears chewed off. Wearing his ever present big smile for me he couldn't get his words out quick enough as he came running into the empty garage.

"Mimi, come see all the Christmas presents we got in the trunk. Daddy says we're gonna go see Papa's grave. Come on, Abby, you have to help carry in some stuff too." Derek rushed back outside to help unload the van. I stood there wondering how to answer him. That has been my worry all along. How were the others, especially the children, coping with Roy's death? It was Shelley, Shane and Abby's turn to give me hugs.

"Mimi, are you gonna put up a Christmas tree?"

"I'm not sure – maybe we should."

"But Mommy said we get to open our Christmas presents after we eat Thanksgiving dinner just like we did last year on Christmas Eve at Great-Grandma Phillips' house."

"Mommy's right. This year we are going to have Christmas at Thanksgiving."

I wonder if this is how Derek would tell the rest of the story.

Papa died in March. I was sick and Abby was too. Daddy took the van with Max to go to Kansas. Abby and I stayed with Mimi Dot and Mommy flew to Wichita on an airplane. When Mommy came back, I had to go to the hospital and Daddy and Max came home. But Mimi stayed by herself in Kansas.

Mimi and Aunt Tootie came to see us in Texas for my birthday in May and after school was over we packed the van to come see Mimi in Kansas. But Papa wasn't there. Mommy says Papa is in heaven.

Max misses Papa. He just walks around sniffing and wants out to look for him outside. Mimi says he can still smell Papa. Daddy took us to the cemetery to see Papa's grave. I don't know why Papa had to die. I wonder how they put him in the ground. Mimi says, "Papa's head is at the end by the headstone with his name."

Last year Christmas was the same way I always remember with Mimi and Papa Phillips. Mommy, Daddy, Abby and I went to Kansas for a whole week. We opened our Secret Santa packages at Great-Grandma and Grandpa's house on Christmas Eve. On Christmas morning at Mimi's our Christmas stockings were full and we got to open more presents. Then the cousins came and we played all over the house. Up and down the basement steps; hiding from each other in the closets. We ate snacks all day. Gun powder dip with taco chips, Chex mix and carrot sticks. Uncle Jason made Rice Krispie cookies and Mommy made chili. Grown-ups played cards and talked and watched TV. Papa and baby Hannah took a nap in Papa's recliner. I did that when I was little. Abby and Krystine did too.

It's not the same now with Papa gone. When we got back this year to Mimi's house from Great-Grandma Phillips', Mimi went down to the laundry room to get the Christmas tree and a red box full of decorations. Daddy put the tree together and Krystine, Abby, Ella and I got to put the decorations on it. Mimi had some old ones just like I make at school. Mimi said my Uncle Jason made them when they were little like us cousins. I wanted to hang them on the tree by myself.

The little Christmas tree didn't have a star so Daddy made one out of paper. And we each got to color a point. Uncle Jason had to help Hannah. Daddy put our initials on each point so Mimi would always remember which one we colored. Daddy wrote, "Merry Christmas Mimi 2002" in the middle and he put it on top of the tree. Mimi cried. I wondered if Papa could see us from heaven. The lights looked just like stars. Mimi cried. So did Aunt Tootie and Great-Grandpa Hager. I think Daddy and Mommy did. I miss Papa. I wish he didn't have to die.

Christmas was Thanksgiving this year. I am glad we could all be together. I am sure that Papa was glad too. But I think he cried.

Icy Obstacles

"Courage doesn't always roar. Sometimes courage is the quiet voice at the end of the day saying, 'I will try again tomorrow.'"
Anonymous

Kansas winters
winds moan
lifeless tree limbs creak and groan
they shudder crashing snow chunks
onto pock-marked white landscape
agglomerating snow fluffs
deepen drifts
and freeze the feelings around my heart.

It starts after Christmas decorations are stored
with the weight of New Year's icy slush.
Leaden sky
suffocates life
threatens budding hope.
A thin sunray sneaks through
as silent reminder
nothing in Kansas stays frozen forever.
Thaw will come again.

    Last weekend the freezing rain turned my driveway into a Teflon ski slope. I had to find a way up that slippery "bunny hill" in order to drive my Saturn L-200 into its safe dry space.

    Crawling on all fours up the hill on the grassy side I finally got into the garage where I discovered "ice melt" crystals in a plastic jug with a handle and holes in the lid and a five-pound bag of potting soil waiting with patient vigilance along the north wall for such a time as this. I shook that jug of miracle melt balls on the concrete out in front of me just like I shake salt on my eggs.

    When the jug was empty, I went back for the potting soil. Continuing my uneasy descent down the slippery driveway I sowed handfuls of dry soil in a hefty arc out in front of me turning the ice black. I felt like I was throwing a sacrifice at the frozen feet of Old Man Winter.

    At the bottom of the drive, with aching arms, I pulled myself back into my ice covered red car sitting crosswise in the middle of the glazed street. Inching forward it was almost too easy to drive up that slope and on into the now cold but dry garage. I put the Saturn in park and breathed a sigh of relief as the garage door rolled down. I was home. I was safe. I would soon be warm.

    In Kansas, as well as on my journey through grief, ice and snow will freeze the landscape again and again. I can't always wait for it to melt on its own.

Gene Blake reflects

Women's work. Men's work. Women cook, clean, and mend. Men take out the garbage, mow the lawn, shovel the snow, and get the oil changed in the car. There was a time when duties around the home were defined this rigidly. Thankfully, we now live in a time of greater flexibility.

Yet most couples establish a division of labor in their relationship. She may mow the lawn and he may vacuum the carpet. This allows each one's skills, abilities, and preferences to be matched to individual responsibilities. Most, if not all, couples work out their plan for dividing up household chores. The process is very efficient, saving time and emotional energy. That is … until one of them dies. Suddenly, survivors find there's a task they don't know how to perform: balancing the checkbook, cooking a meal, doing the laundry, paying bills, etc.

I'm reminded of the time my wife suffered with severe back problems for a month. I needed to learn all sorts of household tasks, like washing dirty clothes and frying eggs. Much to my surprise I learned how to do both and more. But I wasn't in the midst of a grieving process at the time.

A good friend – and very capable woman – surprisingly confessed she had a deathly fear of going into a bank following her farmer-husband's death. He'd always handled that part of their finances. The unfamiliar was frightening in her state of grief.

Often it's challenging and exciting to learn new skills and processes, but not when, we're adjusting to the loss of a loved one. We resist the unfamiliar. Minor tasks suddenly become overwhelming. Emotions boil the surface of our once calm lives. Feelings of helplessness and inadequacy are common. We may even become angry with the deceased for not being there and leaving us alone to struggle with this unwanted responsibility. Or, we may feel guilty for not learning to perform some task when our loved one was alive and could have taught us.

Slowly, we assume additional responsibilities as we learn to function on our own. We might not enjoy the learning process, but we accept it as part of our grief work. We know we are reaching the stage of acceptance when we start to take a little pride in our confidence and independence.

My First-Born Son

No cake to bake. No more presents to buy and wrap. No special evening to plan. This would have been Roy's birthday but since he died how do we celebrate? How does a mother remember when her first-born son dies too soon? Or any child for that matter. Roy had another brother that died shortly after he was born. What is it that mothers remember when birth dates come again, and again? I asked Ruth what she might be thinking today.

It's Roy's birthday. Born sixty years ago at 2:20 a.m. in St. Mary's Hospital in Emporia, Kansas. It was a Friday, February 12, and it was 1943. Roy weighed 6 pounds, 12 ounces. We stayed ten days in the hospital and then Dad left for the army the next day. It was the 23rd of February.

Roy was a good-sized baby when Ray came home on furlough in July from Camp McCain, Mississippi. We took pictures whenever we could in those days. Had to. With the 149th Combat Engineers, Ray was in the initial landing on Omaha Beach, Normandy, France. It was D-Day, June 6, 1944. After a tour in Northern France the Army sent him and two other sergeants back to the states to be shipped to the Pacific landing in Okinawa on D-Day in April, 1945. It's a miracle Roy Richard ever saw his dad again. The times were hard. But it was the same for everyone. The pictures we took show sparse living.

When Sherry called us to meet them at the hospital because "Roy had collapsed in the backyard," the memory of my own dad's dying flashed through my mind. I heard Mom screaming; I'll never forget that sound. Looking out from the south window in my upstairs bedroom, with Roy in my arms, I could see Dad lying on the ground by the grain bin door. Mom kept screaming for help. It was like he just dropped dead to the ground. Roy died the same way. Dad was only forty-nine and it was early Father's Day morning, June 18, 1944. The night before my dad died Roy was riding with him on the old tractor. But Roy had to grow up not knowin' his Granddad Brown.

Roy was a good kid. He was always so responsible. He learned to play the piano and accordion. He taught himself to play the guitar. He loved to sing. Roy was in the Boy Scouts. Ray was a troop leader and I was a den mother. Roy was my den chief. Robert and Ronnie earned their Eagles. Russell was a Cub Scout when Roy's first son, Shane, was born.

Roy was a marvelous son. He always made us so proud. All of our kids have – Robert, Ronnie, Russell and Anne and their families. Can I dare think the blessings outweigh the sad, difficult times?

We all have holes in our lives and broken hearts. I worry about Sherry. We've all got someone but she's the one who goes home to sleep in an empty bed.

Gene Blake reflects

It's been said, "We know we will probably bury our parents. We realize we have about a 50/50 chance of losing our spouse. But we don't expect our children to die before we do."

A couple of decades ago, when I was active in our local hospice, I attended a seminar in a nearby town. The only thing I remember the presenter saying was, "It takes one to two years to cope well following the death of a spouse. But it takes three to five years to deal with the death of a child." The awesome pain of losing a child was brought home to me when I helped a friend start a bereavement support group for parents who had lost children (as she had). One evening our group consisted of 18 people crowded into my large office. All of them had lost a child or, in a few cases, a grandchild. It proved to be the heaviest experience of my ministry.

When one loses a spouse through death, it's easy to forget there are others mourning the same loss. Although it may seem incomprehensible, the spouse's parents, if they are alive and mentally alert, have an even more difficult grieving process. It is their "flesh and blood" who has died – they are burying a part of themselves.

One may think it is a blessing to live a long and fruitful life. And, often it is. But there is also the increased risk of losing a grown child through death. I've seen it happen. The common response is for a parent, like Ruth, to say, "They should be burying me – not Roy."

One very positive thing about Sherry's grieving has been her inclusion of other family members: sons and daughters-in-law, grandchildren, and, especially, Roy's parents. ✤

What Shall I Send?

"With all wisdom and insight God has made known to us the mystery of his will, according to God's good pleasure that God set forth in Christ, as a plan for the fullness of time, to gather all things in him, things in heaven and things on earth."

Ephesians 1:8b-10

And the Lord said to the New Sojourner in Paradise, "What shall I send to her, in this time of loss for you? Tell me what will bring her comfort and courage to keep going into her future of unknowing. What shall I send?"

"The butterfly, a single-engine airplane, and the dove." The New Sojourner spoke with caring and decisiveness after brief, silent contemplation knowing what the One Waiting, as a very real presence, would easily recognize as strength to meet the challenges in the days to come.

"And what is the meaning of butterfly, the small airplane, and dove that will be so readily understood by the One Waiting?" asked the Lord.

New Sojourner explained, "The color, surprise and flight of butterfly will raise her spirits, delight her eye, and give her direction. The sound of airplane flying will lift her eyes heavenward, will encourage her to listen; it will stir memories of our past, and while watching the direction of flight help her to plan with purpose for her future."

"But what of dove?" queried the Lord.

"The coo of dove will be a soft sound to comfort her soul and keep her heart from becoming stone. The dove and its mate will draw a soft smile upon her lips to help heal her broken heart. The dove and its young will assure her of love everlasting. And the friendliness of dove will draw her into tomorrows. The watching eye of dove will speak of closeness and the need to share."

Another question from the Lord, "Will she see the presence of Paradise in these symbols from Creation?"

"Oh, yes!" whispered the New Sojourner as he nodded and winked in his familiar way. "The One Waiting has journeyed with me along the spiritual path. She is a few steps behind and is not yet content with Your Mysteries. But her searching and questions have brought knowledge that life is more than breath and that death is not the end. She taught me the importance, even necessity, of community. I taught her that speaking is not the only way to express presence, caring, concern, and love. She sees the face of Christ in everyone she meets. For her, symbols and signs have always been the assurance of Presence for those who have eyes to see and ears to hear. She seeks and finds meaning in believing that peace is not only planned but also possible and that justice will prevail for all. Be assured, dear Lord, she will know."

"The butterfly of new life and the dove of peace and justice I understand," continued the Lord. "But the airplane is a bit unusual don't you think?"

New Sojourner, showing outward patience, but inwardly feeling the urge to move on, explained to the Lord the small airplane and its flight would symbolize the pilot, passengers, and charted life shared with the One Waiting, with family, with co-workers and friends. After all, this was a major part of his life. But would it be wise to continue this reminder, New Sojourner wondered – but only for a moment.

"You have thought carefully and planned wisely perhaps typical of your engineering vocation and the quiet upbringing which taught you a practical approach to living. Like you, 'I Am' is sure the One Waiting will find comfort and courage with these symbols of faith and love. A chart will be needed for her days to come. Hope is lived out when we believe there is tomorrow and when we plan for morning to dawn. Your choices show wisdom as well as love and will comfort New Sojourner as well as One Waiting. You may now continue your walk into Paradise."

As New Sojourner continued into Paradise, his boots made familiar sounds on the walk. He smiled his quiet smile and gave a knowing wink confident his lover would find the reassurance she needed and feel his presence until they would sojourn together again. He turned toward the days to come that were like early morning light awakening the darkened night.

The One Waiting sat by the beach at Kona, Hawaii, and watched the setting sun give way to a darkening sky. The last reflections of purple-hued orange began to rest on the placid navy blue of the vast expanse of ocean. She sat on the open-air patio of the Hula Bean Café sipping her coffee and was comforted by the peaceful scene. The sound of steps coming along the sidewalk drew her eyes from the horizon to see two lovers walking hand in hand. As they approached her along the cobblestone walk, she noticed his boots. She listened again to their sound and gave a quiet, comforting sigh. "Could this be Paradise?" she wondered.

The colors, depth, and expanse of Paradise required of New Sojourner to pray this day for the ones he knew and who were still waiting. The gentle waves whispered his prayer the next day for ones he did not know. And the charted course of a whale-watching ship waiting for the blow spray of breaching mammals gave directness to pray each third day for any enemies he may have made from first breath until last. Whatever lay ahead was still mystery but New Sojourner was content. Thanks be to God.

Gene Blake reflects

An older woman, a wise story-teller, once shared this bit of wisdom with a young friend, "You're told everything you need to know if you pay attention." But do we pay attention? Are we distracted by the busyness of life: the interruptions, the noise, the onslaught of TV, radio, newspapers, magazines? Do we notice birds, bugs, butterflies, and other bits of nature around us? Only the wise take time to appreciate the complexity and beauty of life on this earth. The prayerful talk to God but seldom listen for or pay attention to that "still small voice."

It's a gift to be intuitive – to be sensitive to the subtle comments and body language of others, to get beyond our selfish concerns, to notice and appreciate the strange coincidences of life, and to be aware of the bigger picture involved in some minor incident. But intuition must be nurtured, trusted, and appreciated. We must be intentional about paying attention.

Likewise, we must pay attention to the lessons of life – lessons large and small. Our faith is a great resource. So are friends, books, and counselors. Even grief has the potential of teaching us important lessons about life and love. Learning is a life-long process. It doesn't stop with our formal education. In fact high school, college, or graduate school just scratch the surface and give us resources. Life's most important lessons are learned from experience – experiences of suffering and failure as well as joy and success.

A Goodbye Letter

February 21, 2003

Dearest Roy,

I am sitting on the beach at Waikiki in Honolulu, Hawaii. I'm on that third trip you and I were planning to take to watch the WSU Shockers play baseball. The Battery Club arrived on the 14th in Kona on the Big Island. The Shocks play a second game at Rainbow, with-a-new-name, Stadium against the University of Hawaii-Honolulu "Bows" at 6:35 p.m.

Basketball games and an endowed scholarship in our names for the College of Engineering are just two of the ways I will continue our support for your alma mater.

Coming here without you is hard but it helps me remember our other trips with the team back in 1999 and 2001. Wasn't it fun to discover we were ready to make these biannual trips a habit? And then we were planning this third trip.

I didn't want to come without you but everyone encouraged me. Even said you would want me to. I guess you would have gone again without me. But here I am and you would be proud of me. I still have my book and my coffee cup trademarks. Can't let everything change.

Our Battery Club friends are good to me. So encouraging. Janis and Kathy helped to endow the Roy R. Phillips Memorial Baseball Scholarship. Memorial monies to the Student Athletic Scholarship Organization from your family, co-workers and friends began what will be a continuing gift to help all of us remember your faithful, enthusiastic support of the Shocker baseball team. The first recipient was announced to us on your birthday, February 12. Incoming freshman, Tommy Hotovy, is a super pitcher with pro potential. Go Shocks!

I had dinner with our friends at Quinn's Fish and Chips before we left Kona last week. We remembered you in your huge black coat and Big Foot boots trying to keep warm while watching early season games with snow on the ground. I'll be wearing that coat myself when we get back to Kansas. We had strawberry margaritas and made a toast to your memory.

I found a real blessing in a used-book shop behind the laundromat on the Big Island at Kona just a block from the hotel. A copy of the book written by Ina Hughes titled, *Prayers for Children* was on the shelf. During a short, hard rain that kept me looking longer I found a book about how to mourn the loss of a spouse and a small handbook on writing. Great bargains for less than $10.

I headed back to the King Kameamea Hotel after the rain stopped and two spectacular Monarch butterflies swooped around and round me as I hopped puddles. The air was cool but my heart was warmed with this sweet, beautiful experience. It was like a surprise wrapped in silvery paper with a golden bow. I know it sounds crazy but I could feel your delight.

This letter is hard to write. But it feels like the best time and place. You and I had such good times here together. Letting go will prepare me to write the next chapters in my life story.

With rising sun, my days with you retreat like the tide. With moonrise, memories of you overtake me like the incoming surf overwhelms the beach one wave at a time. It is the ebb and flow of this eternal sea that I am awash in now. This landscape invites the artist to paint the sunset, hibiscus, sand, and ocean colors of tomorrows to cover the blank canvas of despair. Inspiration for the poet can be heard in the surf and felt in the wind.

The Bengal tiger colors of Monarch butterflies catch my eye. They flutter round attracted by the goldenrod color of my Shocker shirt. Their wings stroke the air and make butterfly kisses like eyelashes on baby cheeks.

Moments like this make me stronger. In the powerful crashing of white-capped waves, I hear your encouraging words, "Go for it, Babe. You won't know if you don't try."

In this paradise where expanse of sea and land meet, I find comfort from the visits of white doves. They join me for just-after-daybreak breakfast on the patio outside my eighth floor hotel room. I drink hot, black coffee and eat a paper-box-bowl full of Cinnamon Chex Squares covered with 2% milk bought the night before from the everywhere-anywhere ABC store. The doves get a few crispy crumbs crunched up and tossed to the concrete. I am sure they are the reassuring presence of your spirit. Their unblinking black eyes stare at me and I wait for them to wink like you used to do when we made eye contact in a crowd.

It is that same skin-sense I had when the small airplanes flew over the ball field on Kona when the Shockers played Hilo and again when that paper-white butterfly flew along beside me on my daily walk across the back lot to the ball field.

Dear Roy – lover, partner, my friend – saying goodbye holds such sweet sorrow. This is my chance to say, "Bye Babe," one last time.
Love,
Me

Damn You, Roy Richard Phillips

I stepped out of the car into ankle deep snowy slush in the parking lot at Town West Mall. It was a cloudy, gloomy day during a depression that seemed to erase the positive steps I made getting through the holidays of that first year. It was February 26, two weeks after Roy's birthday and eleven months after his death. The sound of an unseen single-engine airplane flying somewhere overhead triggered this blast of anger directed at Roy for dying too soon. I sloshed my way into the mall, headed straight to the food court, and sat down to write.

Dear Babe,
Look what you've gone and done. You left me! I am in a mess, a great big mess.

All you said when I left was "Bye, Babe." Just your usual send off. When I got home you were supposed to have the yard mowed, the leaves raked, and trees trimmed. The mower should have been in the garage, your drink jug fresh with ice and Diet Rite. You should have been showered, napped, and ready for dinner out with our Wichita kids: Jason and Kristen and grand girls, Krystine and Hannah. That was the deal; that was our plan.

It was the promise we always made – to see each other in just a bit. I know. I know. I left without saying it. I started to go back into the house to tell you, believe me I did. But my hands were full of stuff to take to the recycle warehouse and the clock was running. I needed to go to the mall to buy birthday cards. I had those two damn-important errands and too little time to take two more seconds to go back into the house and holler down the stairs at ya, "Bye, Babe" just like we always did.

You left us all without a word of goodbye. Damn you, Roy Richard Phillips. How could you do that? You should have done what we planned. I know you loved us. How could you just fall down and die without telling us so we could be with you? You could have called me on your cell phone. You could have called your folks. You could have at least punched in 911. Damn you, Roy. Oh, damn you, Babe!

You died and left. Left me in a mess. The paperwork, the phone calls, the magazines piling up, again. Checks to write; money to invest. It's a mess, my desk. And our hearts – oh, our hearts are still in shreds.

It was always my stuff waiting to be done. All of our household affairs filed neatly in your office downstairs and my church files upstairs and papers stacked all over my desk. But now I get the whole damn business because you up and died. Damn you, Roy, oh, damn you.

I know, I know. You and the good Lord sent butterflies and doves, and those damned single-engine airplanes. I've seen so many little airplanes I can tell a Cessna from a Beech. You'd never believe that or maybe you'd be proud of me.

It is cloudy again today and it's been gloomy for weeks. My days seem dark as navy nights and it's noon. I hear another airplane I cannot see. You must be flying above the clouds warm in the sunshine and probably enjoying paradise. Damn you, Roy.

At home the mail is piled up, the *Wichita Eagle* newspapers stacked and waiting to tell me of all the tragedy that happened here while I was away.

Away? You're asking me, "Did I go away?" You're damned right I went away. I took that trip, our trip. That third trip we were supposed to take together to Hawaii to watch the Shocker baseball team have fun in the warm-as-melted-butter sunshine doing what they love – playing baseball in 80-degree weather in February. Eighty degrees. Baseball and sunburns. You bet I was away!

Good folks, super food, wonderful weather, calm seas, and I sitting lonely on a crowded Waikiki beach. "No laptops allowed here in Paradise." "Are you going to sing playing that keyboard?" questioned the locals. I was the odd one. Everyone else relaxed in the close-to-the-equator winter.

I could see surfers far out from shore, treading water, waiting without a care in the world for the next big wave. With the coming spring pushing the calendar and coaxing the pink and yellow hibiscus buds from sap-enriched limbs, I watched as gardeners trimmed magnolia trees around the hotel parking lot.

New life all around me reminding me of the day you died almost a year ago. It was too-early spring then too and extra warm. That memory is as fresh as clear salt air.

I came home from the mall to find you had yanked dead leaves from the yucca and trimmed the juniper trees too high again. You must've been hell-bent pushing round and round that mower mulching up sycamore leaves from trees down the street. It's hot, dry, dusty work thatching our 30-year-old Bermuda grass lawn. Four hours of work almost done. Just a few more rounds of the back yard left to be mowed. I saw you when I looked out the kitchen window. You were slumped down against the fence.

Hell-bent to get everything done that you could for the boys and me. Hell-bent to get that early spring lawn cleanup done. You didn't have that much time, did you? Our good neighbor, Mr. Hong, said you were too busy mowing to stop and talk with him like you always did. He said you looked tired. You were dying weren't you? Did it hurt? What about that little bit of indigestion you had when you came home from your two-hour choir practice? Did it get worse? What about numbness in your arms? Didn't you have any warning to stop, to take that cell phone off your belt and call for help?

I told 911 I couldn't tell if you were breathing. Half sitting, half reclining on the ground by the backyard chain link fence you were protected by just enough spring growth to hide you from the neighbors' sight. It looked like you sat down to rest and just fell asleep.

It seemed so dumb – you were listening to your radio strapped on your arm with plugs in your ears. Did you hear the ambulance sirens? I was so glad we were close to the hospital. I told them to come straight to the back yard, where to look for the house numbers above the garage. I knew they needed to get there fast. And they did.

I heard their words as the worked, I hear them now, but I was busy dialing the phone to call Jason at work and your folks.

But, damn you, Roy, you died anyway.

Dr. Keller told me weeks later that you wouldn't have felt a thing. No pain. Death takes just a few minutes with cardiac arrhythmia. The words eased my heart.

You'd paid the bills for March. You had the taxes figured and filed so early the refunds were already in the bank – ready to pay for the funeral. I was glad for that.

I guess I had my, "Bye, Babe" earlier. I remember saying to you as you sat on the edge of the bed pulling on work jeans, "I think we've been married almost too long." You smiled and asked what I meant. "I love you so much. I'm going to miss you when you're gone." With your head on my chest you gave me a tender hug. Did you have any gut feeling about what was going to happen? Did I? Why didn't I know something was wrong?

You were ready as much as anyone possibly could be for meeting death. No mystery concerned you. You were successful. Happy, healthy, wealthy by any standard. Grandkids young and ripe for our influence and involvement in their lives. Hell, we're still young. But, damn you, Roy, I was supposed to die first.

Were you just listening to that Shocker double header at Evansville? Or were you thinking, "I have to get this done before I die. I wish I could take time to call Shane and Shelley and to talk to Derek and Abby once more. Why can't death wait until after dinner with Jason and Kristen and the girls tonight?" Did you wish I had been there? And what about your folks? What are they going to do?

No blood, no bruises. No call for help. Damn you, Roy. You left me in such a mess.

Gene Blake reflects

Anger – it's probably the most difficult emotion to face and deal with in the process of grieving. It's common to feel anger and also to feel guilty for feeling angry – especially the anger we feel toward the deceased or God. It just doesn't seem socially acceptable or appropriate. Yet it's real.

This anger may be rational or irrational. If the deceased didn't take care of his or her health, took part in some risky behavior, or made no financial preparation for an untimely death, then rational anger is more than understandable. A drunken driver may have veered across some centerline or a medical professional may have made some serious mistake. It's not difficult to see why these would make a person angry.

Irrational anger is probably more common. We're angry because of this drastic change in our life. Usually we're angry at the deceased for leaving us alone or God for taking our loved one. Since we don't feel right about these feelings we often dump our anger on innocent people: Emergency medical personnel, nurses, or doctors who "should have tried a little harder," family members, funeral directors, those with whom we must work to change insurance records, legal papers, retirement accounts, real estate titles, etc. Or those who try to express their condolences with inaccurate or insensitive comments and theologies: "I know how you feel." "You'll find someone new." "God must have needed another angel." "You can have another child." "He's in a better place now."

But how should we deal with this anger that is oh so real? Probably the best alternative is to be part of a bereavement support group where we can express our feelings to people who understand. Talking is healing. But not everyone is receptive to hearing our story over and over again. Most friends and family members just aren't up to it. We must keep in mind members of our family may also be dealing with the same loss.

Journaling or writing may help us put our anger into words rather than into someone's face. However we work through this difficult issue, we must avoid suppressing the hostility we feel. Suppressed anger turns into depression and stalls the grieving process. And, the deceased may understand as well.

An End to the First Year

"The only cure for grief is action."
George Henry Lewes

The countdown begins today. Thursday, Friday, Saturday and Sunday. These early spring days, just like last year, have begun to march into my mind again like U.S. soldiers marching into Iraq late yesterday repeating the Gulf War of a decade ago. Like a bad dream that is persistent and disturbs what once was a peaceful routine of sleep March 21, 22, 23, and 24 of 2002, have returned to haunt my days.

Thursday before Roy died on Saturday was that awful day of the toilet running over after his morning "session". The downstairs bathroom was his peaceful refuge from my first-thing-in-the-morning habit of talking as soon as I got out of bed. But that morning the sewage-lift pump died and a backup from hell overflowed at the inconvenient hour of 7:00 a.m. – Roy's scheduled time to leave for work.

Shut off the water and grab the wet vac while wife calls a plumber was the immediate response. Water disasters in our downstairs had become a habit. But last year's was particularly nasty. Roy, dressed in business suit, white shirt, and tie, did what he could then left for the scheduled early morning meeting with his staff.

By 10:30 a.m. he was home talking with the plumber about replacing the dead sump pump and I was on the phone scheduling the carpet cleaners to clean and disinfect on Friday. As a disaster recovery team we worked well together. We were experienced.

This year my water disaster was discovered late afternoon Monday. A quick trip downstairs to the laundry room to drop a couple of dirty throw rugs into the washer had me walking on water. The carpet in the hall was boggy. I stepped into the bathroom and could see the leak from the underside of the toilet tank. I shut off the water and called the insurance agent.

I was lucky to find Martin in the office. He knew Roy was dead and said, "Sherry you're going to need a disaster clean up company but it shouldn't cost as much as your deductible so go ahead and give 'em a call yourself."

The fans and dehumidifier are running full blast downstairs as I journal about this year's water nightmare repeating history, like round two of the Gulf War. I write this story not just to repeat history. It is healthy remembering. Learning from experience what to do. Knowing who I can count on. It is about my growing through the yo-yo of living. Life is so darn unpredictable. It is about proving I can get through these next few days in order to live into the days that follow.

First, I had to accept the nightmare was real. Roy's body was in the grave. His life was celebrated with more than 500 witnesses. But that was last year.

These new anniversaries will be counted as the "woulda, coulda, shoulda's." In February, Roy would have been sixty years old. Coming this June we could have been married for forty years.

This first year of "firsts" is almost over. What about seconds and thirds? Sounds like passing plates at the dinner table.

Was that a joke? Not really but at the end of this first year I am beginning to see in more than black and white, to feel something besides numbness and cold, to hear laughter from my own lips, while I try to find meaning in this new kind of life. I'm not ready to move on like some people talk about getting over the death of their spouse. But I know each day is another chance for things to feel better.

In the grief support group, we talk about grief not dealt with will come back to haunt. I don't want nightmares to overshadow my life with Roy which was like a dream come true. Roy's not coming back. My journey from the past has to turn into a journey facing my future. A journey to what, I do not know. I just know that it's up to me to keep plodding along.

Gene Blake reflects

Shortly after Roy's death I told Sherry, "Eventually you'll have to reinvent yourself." In the process of grieving we establish a new identity. It may not be significantly different from our old self, but in many basic ways who we are changes. We're no longer someone's spouse and more than any married person realizes their identity is tied to their relationship as husband or wife.

Many who are newly widowed find it difficult to mark themselves as single on forms and documents. The act is more symbolic than one would think. But being single or married is a part of our identity.

Our circle of friends also changes. We find ourselves feeling uncomfortable around couples – even though they may be old friends. Sometimes couples actually exclude us – possibly because they feel uncomfortable around us. Old friends don't know what to say, consequently they don't say anything and contact is lost.

I also told Sherry she would be surprised by people whom she thought were good friends, but would prove otherwise. Likewise, I told her there were people who would become better friends and be supportive of her, also to her surprise. During the grieving process understanding, accepting friends are a tremendous asset. Their support is invaluable.

Early in the grieving process it seems as if survival is the only achievable goal we can set for ourselves. At times that may even seem questionable. But, as the proverb says, "Time heals." However, I would add, "It's usually not time alone." Support groups, counselors, clergy, listening friends, study, etc. are also necessary for healthy grieving.

Some people "get stuck in their grief." They go through the rest of their lives without working through the loss of a loved one. How sad!

Some experts divide the grieving process into stages. One of the last stages is acceptance. It's a time when life takes on a new normalcy – when the emotional pain is no longer intense and we spend more time looking forward rather than back. It's a time when the future seems to hold some hope and we have a growing comfort with our new identity.

Once we accept our situation and realize we are going to survive – even with a new identity – our next goal is to feel as if we are truly living.

We must decide what new challenges and opportunities to embrace, what to leave behind, and figure out how to create new meaning and purpose in life. This can be both exciting and frightening. Our future may look uncertain, but we're forced to admit it always has been. We just didn't realize it. That's one of the great lessons of grief. ✤

Reminders

A verse on a decorative plaque and music box that plays, *Wind Beneath my Wings,* catches my eye while I wait at Tillie's Flower Shop:

> "A butterfly lights beside us and for a brief moment
> its splendor and beauty are part of our world.
> Eventually it flies away and even though we wish it would have stayed
> we feel fortunate for what it brought us."
> Katy Fuher

a year ago you died
lives shattered, hearts broke
gone a year – yet only a breath away
memories I hear and feel are puzzle pieces
voice, laughter, wisdom
your boots across the floor
        hugs, head scratches, hands holding, massage of shoulders and feet
reminders come in symbols
        butterfly, the sound of airplane, the sight of mourning doves
responses to
cries for guidance
pleas for courage
        heartbreaking loneliness
Before you died
I knew the house would feel too big

The lawn more than I would want to water or mow
A year ago you died
The house feels too small when all the family comes home
Someday the lawn will be landscaped with rock and butterfly bushes
Mourning doves coo –
"Remember, Babe, I love you."

This Day Is too Hard

sun reflects like gold in candlelight
spring colors make pastel splotches in surprising places
imagine a flower shop
a sour feeling in my stomach
bitter taste of loss lingers like a sip of spoiled milk
card is colorful like Mardi Gras
flowers fill in the front like doodle drawings made with felt pens
I know the sender knows what this day is like
her journey a few months longer than mine
phone rings just in time
pulls me back from the brink of depression
the caller understands my ups and downs
friendships solid as limestone boulders half buried in a Cowley County quarry.

This day is too hard, so was yesterday, as will be tomorrow. And the next day. Since Roy's death nothing seems to work the first time. "Take one day, one thing at a time" is the mantra of grievers. But why does everything have to be done over and over to get it right.

    My seed catalog is more like a weed catalog of feelings. It is full of frustration, sadness, anger, bitterness. I am overwhelmed, lost, out of control, vulnerable. The list smothers my creativity. It is like bindweed encircling its way up the chain link fence until it reaches low branches of the redbud tree next door and begins to pull at and contort the limbs. I just want to be able to snap free of this burden. I need to be free to breathe.

Dare I take my portable office tote bag with bills to pay and mail to read and head once more for Java Villa? A bierock with fruit salad and chips plus a Mother Jones diet black cherry soda will cut me loose for awhile. Maybe after lunch I can mail the bills and stop off at Genesis Health Club. Lifting weights, stretching muscles, pumping up heart rate could help me be stronger for tomorrow.

Is This Normal?

The Merry Maids crew will be here tomorrow. Last week I had to admit I am still not able to stick to one task long enough to get anything really done. With Shane, Derek, and Abby coming this Friday I know I need more help. Hiring someone to do the routine "grunt" work of dusting, run the vacuum and scrub the tub seems a sensible alternative.

Even now trying to put stuff out of sight so the surfaces will be reachable for the cleaners bogs me down. I feel guilty because I have put off so much for so long. Is this normal?

Everything I touch reminds me of Roy or something else – my travels or work with the church, our trips for baseball and vacations. His toys – electronic gizmos, CD's, lawn and garden tools, computer games and video recordings are everywhere. My necessities are organizers, pens, papers, files, books, conference notes. The memories are wrapped up in the excess – a testimony to living an upper middle-income lifestyle for over 20 years.

My stuff is too much. His stuff is the tangible remains of his personhood ... engineer, pilot, music lover and bass singer, and fanatic fan of the Wichita State University Shockers basketball and baseball teams. Yardman, fixer-upper, mechanic, and saver. He always knew that a screw, tool, leftover paint, paper, and glue would be, could be, used again.

This recycler par excellence rubbed off on me and I love to keep giveaway stuff – promo items from all those conferences fill my desk, shelves and filing cabinets along with old reports and new resources from two years ago.

This guilt I am feeling comes from watching the Home and Garden television channel while I eat my supper downstairs in the family room. Too many "Clean Sweep," and "Mission Organization" reruns have convicted me no end. I don't believe my house looks like any they show on TV but the formula is the same for a little or a lot. Remove everything from the room then sort – toss, sell, give away, or keep. The other handy part is that more than one does the work. And the taskmaster keeps a sharp eye questioning many decisions and helping with willpower to pare down in order to organize a little rather than a lot.

The plan makes sense. But it is this weight I get in my chest when I open a drawer and see his things. I still feel the need to pick them up, hold them close and after the lump in my throat goes away return the item to its nest.

Is this normal?

※

Gene Blake reflects

Is it normal to question our normality? Certainly! This is quite common during the grieving process. Society – and often our family and friends – gives us two to three weeks for a process which can consume that same number of years. Insensitive comments about "getting on with life" are bound to make us question whether we're normal or stuck in a black hole of grief.

Most people own a lot of stuff which is an integral part of their lives. When loved ones die they leave behind many things we associate with their memory. It's normal for these items to provoke what seem like abnormal emotions.

Inherent in most of us is the tendency to measure ourselves against some nebulous standard of what other people are like and how they behave. Am I more or less attractive? Intelligent? Energetic? Creative? Do I behave in a normal fashion or am I a little weird? Implicit in all these questions is this subtle but significant one: "What do other people think of me?"

Grieving requires courage – courage to accept what we are experiencing and to call it normal. Generally it is unhealthy to allow others (except experienced counselors) to tell us how to grieve. It may cause us to suppress a normal process or to be ashamed of our feelings. On the other hand, being part of a bereavement support group can be quite helpful. It's a place where we can tell our story over and over again to people who understand. Most people who have lost a loved one are keenly aware that good listeners are rare. If they exist among our family and friends we are really lucky. But counselors, clergy, and clinical psychologists are usually trained to give us their attention and to listen to feelings as well as words. Sometimes we need an authority figure to tell us, "What you're experiencing is normal."

Pickup

It was just a pickup. It didn't take thirty minutes. Come and gone. Easy. Refreshing in a way. I breathe deep. I feel alive – I am surprised.

I am not supposed to feel like this. Tears and guilt are brief visitors. But the load lifting from my mind makes my heart pound and pulse hurry. I am exhilarated but exhausted.

Friends came from the church and stood waiting for me to tell them it was okay – okay to load my donation of some of Roy's garage stuff for their garage sale.

Waiting on the shelves and in the corners were the bird feeders, a couple of grass trimmers and two extra packages of plastic twine. The guys started loading it all onto the bed of that old pickup. Twenty-pound bags of concrete mix. Fishing poles. A five-gallon bucket of antifreeze. The red plastic gasoline can for the lawn mower that Jason moved to his garage last summer sloshed still half full of gas. Roy's old boots and a pair of tennis shoes he wore for yard work. All waiting for me to let go. Garden tools and an old red snow shovel. Three extra picnic jugs and a box of old, raggedy tee shirts. Roy's first bowling ball, the boot box full of plumbing elbows, joints, plugs, and seals; the Del Monte grocery box full of electrical wiring, switches, plugs.

His old green toolbox the boys got him for Christmas filled over the years with nails and screws will remain in its place on the workbench. Roy had touched and sorted each screw by size, length, and diameter, the Phillips head from straight cut. His big tool box full of wrenches, pliers, screwdrivers needed through the years to repair, build or maintain our house and cars will stay. He had changed the oil and filter in the Chevy's and Honda's every 5,000 miles.

The old metal bread box with drawers for coffee, tea, flour, and sugar full of 35 years of accumulated odd parts to sort through when he needed to fix, adapt, or build new something, anything. No matter what needed to be done Roy would try to do it. Anything for the house, or car or yard, bicycles, toys, small appliances. The harvest gold can opener unable to open a can for twenty years sits on the workbench as if Roy will use it to sharpen my knives one more time.

The one car attached garage is full of this man. I hear the echo of his old C.B. radio always announcing ambulance and police calls while he sawed and hammered, drilled, screwed, and glued.

Some things have been loaded and hauled away. Thank God the memories get to stay.

Dust makes me sneeze. I reach for the Kleenex and head back into the house to place on paper another story about my healing.

Gene Blake reflects

How and when do we dispose of the possessions left behind when someone dies? Clothes are probably the most personal ... and most difficult item. Do we immediately pack them up for a local charity? Do we put off the decision for so long we somehow feel guilty? Do we keep a favorite sweater that still retains the odor unique to the deceased?

About a decade ago a good friend died shortly after I resigned as pastor of his church. His widow chose to give me some of his very nice dress clothes – some of which I still wear. Although I felt awkward about doing so, I honored her desires. Giving the deceased's clothing to a family member or friend may be one's choice.

I also remember a widow in one pastorate who immediately disposed of all her late husband's possessions and moved to another state. I couldn't help feeling troubled by her decision.

The following article was written by a friend, Susan Freeman, shortly after she'd been widowed. It subtly tells how she dealt with some items of clothing.

Empty Shoes

Medium, size 8½, different colors, shapes, and styles line a wall of her closet. Most are leather, some canvas, a few rubber, even one sheepskin. They are the last items she dons to begin the day, the first she sheds to end it.

Shoes are foot vehicles marking the time-line of man. Who wore the first ones? Did the Leakeys overlook a fossilized shoe print in the Great Rift Valley? Written chronicles describe the foot gear of the ancients. Jesus' feet were wrapped in palm frond sandals, his footprints obscured by desert winds. Fourteen centuries pass and foot armor of the Crusaders following his steps, is now viewed in museums. Bound by dynasty tradition, the slippers of a Chinese woman measure no more than 3½ inches. European aristocrats wore the first pointed toe, high-heeled shoes. A fashion class statement, these shoes weren't meant for walking. Military boots continue to march through the 21st century redefining borders, wearing out hearts.

We bronze baby's first shoes. We are told not to judge a person until we have walked in their shoes. But if the shoe fits, wear it. Cinderella's did and she got her prince. Dorothy found her way home.

There are four pairs of shoes in his closet, nothing else. They are all in a row, dress shoes first, favored sandals last. She cannot bear to part with them. Empty, unmoving, never again to leave a print on her time-line. *(Quoted with permission)*

There's no right or wrong way to deal with the loved one's possessions. And, there's no hurry in deciding what to do. It's okay to take some time. ✿

Twenty Months

It was time to count again. April then May, June, July, August, September, October, and November. Eight months plus one year adds up to 20 months. I look at my fingers in disbelief. Twenty months.

I say to his mother, "It has been twenty months today. How can that be?" In her quiet, solid way she asserts, "Sometimes it seems like years. And then it can feel like March 22nd was yesterday. What day was it Roy died?" She pauses and looks at me through wistful eyes. I take my napkin to catch tears before they make rivulets down my cheeks and then turn my head to look out the window.

Today was Sunday but that day, March 23, 2002, was a Saturday. The death certificate said he died at 4 p.m.

The rain splashes hard on parked cars lined up and looking like cold birds on a telephone wire. The water rushes to the low center of the concrete drive making a shallow creek for folks to navigate as they hurry back to transportation and try to stay dry.

Ruth and I were in the restaurant of the Quality Inn Motel, with our half bananas, breakfast muffins, donuts and coffee. It was late for us – almost seven forty-five in the morning. Packing to head home had slowed us up. But the rain started early – before six. It was the first dismal weather on a short, four-day bus trip from Wichita, Kansas, to see Christmas in Branson, Missouri, and Silver Dollar City.

My mind sees next month and real Christmas without him again. All too soon it will be twenty-four months since Roy's death. I look at my fingers and accept reality.

Gene Blake reflects

During the process of grieving there are occasions when days and months seem eternal – times when we think we will never be whole again. We feel as if we are taking a "time out" from life – other peoples lives are going on, why not ours? We are stuck in grief as a car gets stuck in a snowdrift. The coldness is there as well. We yearn for the warmth of our loved one. We yearn to be free of the ache in our hearts that keeps us stuck at some arbitrary time in our existence.

Yet, on other days, it seems as if the death we mourn occurred in some ancient time – a time so long ago. We struggle to reinforce our memories – we fear we may forget. What day of the week was it? What time? Who was there? What had we done that morning? Was the sky clear or as cloudy as our days seem now?

Friends who have also traveled this difficult road tell us, "The holidays are the most difficult!" There is the empty chair as we gather for Thanksgiving dinner. There's lots of conversation, but no one mentions their name. There's no one with whom to make festive plans. If we travel, we may travel alone. If we stay home the house seems strangely vacant – like a house where we once laughed and loved but do so no more. Who will help decorate the Christmas tree or put up the outside lights? Gifts won't be exchanged. Cherished traditions have lost their meaning. Attempts to start new ones, encounter disappointment. It's a "season of joy" – but not in our hearts.

We often make connections between our environment and emotions. Short, cloudy days bring on depression. Rain reminds us of our easy tears. Stars and planets lighting a night sky connect us to an eternal creation, yet make us feel small and insignificant. We search for meaning and purpose as a child looks for missing pieces in a jigsaw puzzle. We try to put our lives back together but can't seem to find the right plan.

Widow Woes: A Chronicle

Two weeks after the funeral a benign breast lump is removed. Roy's Mom is holding my hand when I wake up.

Hail storm in May has me consulting an insurance adjuster and negotiating with old friends at Southwestern Remodeling for a new roof plus window screen and siding repairs.

Dishwasher quits working in middle of summer. Paper plates and plastic silverware work until ... Everyone is coming for Thanksgiving so I head to Sears for a new Kenmore. It is a lot quieter than the old one.

Shane helps me pick out a new laptop then sets up and installs software transferring data from the old one. He helps move my stuff into Roy's old office space downstairs.

Ice maker freezes up. Sears service blames the cheaper way it was made. He gets creative and fashions a replacement part to make it work the way "they used to."

Contract signed for routine fall and spring maintenance on central heating and air.

My dad's wife leaves him and files for divorce. Depression sinks in. My sister, Sheryl, and I find ourselves fulltime caregivers.

National Disaster and Recovery called when the downstairs toilet tank springs a leak. Mold bloom removed.

In May, Dad's kidney is removed; his last living sibling dies in June. Then my longtime friend, Janice, loses her four-year battle with ovarian cancer. In August while we are in Texas with Sheryl visiting Shane and his family, Dad dies early in the morning in our motel suite – three weeks before his divorce was final. Now his wife is contesting his will.

At home I find the Teflon lining of ice maker peeling leaving chunks in ice cubes. I buy and have installed a new one with extended warranty.

Hot water heater just keeps water warm. With two months left on the ten-year warranty, I head to Sears, again, for a new one. But the new water heater will only have a two-month warranty so I pay extra for an extended warranty.

Ice maker freezes up but service call is no charge. Glad I extended the warranty.

Bathroom sink faucet drips. Plumber takes all morning to install new handles.

Dripping sound at 10 p.m. alerts me to standing water under bathroom sink. A plumber tightens the new faucet handle fitting. No charge for the emergency service call.

Microwave dies. I measure and go shopping right away. Best Buy has the best buy. Jason puts it in and Roy's Dad will salvage metal from the old one.

Handle on upstairs toilet breaks. I call a different plumber to install new "innards" I buy at Home Depot.

Two years after he dies a settlement is reached on Dad's estate. Four attorneys get half, my expenses are reimbursed and three heirs divide what's left.

Beth from grief group offers to show me how to caulk around the bathtub tile. I lose my nerve and call a handyman service. He cleaned the rain gutters too.

Woes happen. We are always grieving to some extent. And knowing what to do, how to do it, or who to call right after the panic subsides is the big lesson. I have learned to rely on folks who know what they are doing, are licensed, bonded, and insured. And I have found I can get creative.

I am thankful I do not have leaking basement walls or sump pump problems. Everyone in the grief group has a litany of woes.

❁

Gene Blake reflects

Like Roy, my bachelor's degree was in mechanical engineering. For 14 years I worked for manufacturing companies writing specifications, designing machinery, purchasing, and installing equipment, writing computer programs, selling products, etc. Inherent in all these engineering activities was one common thread: solving problems.

After being ordained as a Presbyterian minister I found a subtle shift in my professional role. It was no longer my responsibility to solve peoples' problems. Instead, it was my calling to be supportive of others as they solved their own problems. Empathetic listening replaced action. Granted, there have been times I've been tempted to deal with the problem rather than the person, but it wasn't a mistake I made very often.

Sherry's list of woes sounds very familiar. I've listened to her frustrations about most of them – just as she has listened to frustrations about issues related to my health.

Throughout life we encounter problems with vehicles, household appliances, home maintenance, health, and the loss of friends. We each react in our own way. But when we've lost a spouse our reaction is amplified and our threshold of frustration is lowered. What once were manageable problems suddenly become overwhelming obstacles. That's an aspect of grieving.

It's a wise widow who discerns two types of assistance are needed: someone who can solve our workaday problems and someone who will listen to us rant and rave about the reality of grief. ✿

A Time for Everything

*"There is a time for everything,
and a season for every activity under heaven…"*
Ecclesiastes 3:1-7

A Time to Be Born
May 19, 1943, just six weeks after Daddy boarded a bus for boot camp the hospital stamped my birth certificate. Mom and I came home to her folk's house from St. Francis in an ambulance. I was four years younger than my half-sister, Barbara Jean, who had an eight-year-old brother named Billy James Junior. Mom's first husband was a baker. He made bread. On Fridays, he would cash his paycheck, play cards, and shoot craps.

My sister, Sheryl, was born 365 days after I was – in the leap year of '44. I called her Too Too. Most folks thought we were twins.

A Time to Die
My Momma passed away in 1994 at age 79. She had lived seven good years in the Presbyterian Manor. Momma always said she didn't want to be old. For her, 80 would have been old.

My husband turned 59 a month-and-a-half before he slumped to the ground while mowing our backyard and died as they put him in the ambulance. His 83-year-old parents were waiting for us at the hospital. Granddaughter, Krystine, almost 5 years old, hugging me gently, patting my shoulder said through tears of her own, "Everything will be okay. Papa is in heaven with God."

A Time to Tear Down
Dad walked out on Mom when I was a senior in high school. Negotiating the divorce happened in a courtroom.

A Time to Build
Roy and I met at the Deluxe Lanes Bowling Alley on north Washington Street in Wichita, Kansas. He was night manager. I bowled on a team from the ad agency where I worked. He did college homework, smoked Lucky Strikes, and drank black coffee while waiting to set pins or retrieve stuck bowling balls.

Married within a year, then a baby, ten more years of college going part time, and adding another son. I sold Avon and volunteered in the church. Working his way up at Cessna Aircraft Company Roy began unloading railroad cars at the warehouse on Orient Boulevard. Our sons worked their way through Wichita State and have families of their own.

A Time to Mourn
Grief is hard work. I did what I had to do in shock for the first three months. One morning in the dark I admitted Roy was not in Europe or on business in Phoenix. He was dead. In the emptiness of my home and heart I asked out loud, "What do I do now?"

Take one day at a time. Put one foot in front of the other. Take care of myself. This is still my mantra. I joined Good Grief and have found ways to tell my story until I no longer feel the compulsion to regurgitate it.

A Time to Dance
When supportive friends come to a dinner party you host for your 60th birthday fourteen months after your lover dies. When you hear Lee Ann Womack sing, *I Hope You Dance*. And when you discover you can, even without a partner.

A Time to Search
When what is lost needs to be found: a left shoe, the blank-four domino. When questions have no easy answers. When you find yourself single after living coupled most of your life. And long before life has no meaning at all.

A Time to Give Up
Before losing more than you would gain by continuing the pursuit Before someone else has to make those choices for you. And when you discover that to die is to gain.

A Time to Mend
Mending to me is sewing back on a button. I have a jacket that has waited a season for me to get out a needle and thread. Last week I found a button under the workbench, behind my husband's toolbox. The shirt it belonged to is long gone to a Goodwill store. This makes me think of Rebecca. We used to be such good friends…

❈

Gene Blake reflects

Ecclesiastes 3 is a common funeral scripture – I've used it dozens of times. However, I've found the passage sums up most of our lives. The times and cycles of life do include: being born and dying, planting and harvesting, tearing down and building up, weeping and laughing, mourning and dancing, keeping and throwing away, times of silence and speaking, loving and hating.

Yet I've always wondered what the author meant by "a time to throw away stones and a time to gather stones together." However, being aware of the earthiness of the early Jewish authors, I think I know what was meant by "a time to embrace, and a time to refrain from embracing."

Ecclesiastes is part of what's called the "wisdom literature" of the Old Testament. The third chapter, indeed, does contain considerable wisdom and an eternal quality. This is summed up in later verses: "God has made everything suitable for its time; moreover he has put a sense of past and future into their minds, yet they cannot find out what God has done from the beginning to the end. I know that there is nothing better for them than to be happy and enjoy themselves as long as they live."

Implicit in most of the goals grieving people set for themselves is "contentment" – the acceptance of ourselves and our situation. But contentment is counter-cultural in our society. Competition, achievement, wealth, power, control, and recognition come much closer to describing our values and priorities. But they are of little comfort during the grieving process.

It's quite common for a grieving person to endlessly struggle with what's been called the "if onlys."

- If only I'd stayed home, rather than run those errands, maybe we could have saved Roy.
- If only I'd had the opportunity to say, "Goodbye."
- If only I'd encouraged him to see a doctor earlier.
- If only I'd been a better husband, wife, etc.

The list is not only endless, it is also universal. We have far less control over life events than we realize. We can't perfect our lives, our relationships, our society, or the significant events of life. There is a time for everything – some are positive, some aren't.

The *Serenity Prayer* has become quite meaningful to me in these later years. It goes like this: "God grant me the serenity to accept the things I cannot change, courage to change the things I can, and the wisdom to know the difference." I believe this prayer is also very appropriate for the grieving person. We can't change the death of a spouse, but we can muster the courage to join a bereavement group.

Many of the life goals we set for ourselves can only be achieved indirectly. We can't will ourselves to be contented. It is the product of patient self-nurture as we slowly work through the grieving process with the aid of others.

Memories Found in a Bottom Drawer

I discovered a half-used writing tablet in the bottom of a desk drawer on March 9, 2004. It contained the lost log I had started a few days after everyone had gone home after Roy died.

March 23, 2002 – Saturday
Roy was found about 3:20 p.m. by the south fence in the backyard. Unable to revive him he was pronounced dead about 3:50 p.m.

Jason, Kristen, Sheryl, Steve, Ruth and Ray, Frank Blain and Ron Blain, my dad, Gene Hager and his wife, Lil, and Pastor Dennis Winzenried arrived at St. Joseph Hospital almost before the body of Roy. Calls to Shane and others began. Pastor Dennis and the chaplain plus nurse, Cindy, were very helpful.

Police were sent to survey the backyard and the coroner questioned me about the circumstances to be sure that Roy's unattended death was not an accident. We just knew that one whole part of our lives was gone from us and life would never be the same again.

We donated Roy's organs. By midnight those gifts were on their way to help save the lives of others. The Red Cross facilitated all of the process. (They reported later that bone, skin and connective tissue were successfully used in three recipients.)

The folks went to tell Anne and then on home to call the others.

After arriving home food was shared along with tears and memories. Shane called before 9 p.m. from Austin, Texas. It was cruel to tell him, Shelley, Derek, and Abby by phone that Papa had gone so quickly from our lives.

Jason stayed the night after visits from Gene and Mary Blake, Stan and Sue Nispel, Ron, Barbara and Jody Phillips.

March 24 – Sunday
Steve, Sheryl, Jason, Kristen, Krystine, Hannah, and I went to 11 a.m. church to worship God and hear the Palm Sunday cantata sung by the choir and dedicated to Roy's memory. Hearing Pastor Dennis share the news was so hard and comfort only came with prayers for us all.

Home began a parade of food and visitors, phone calls and a repeat of the horror of yesterday. Janice Munds, Rebecca New, Marty

Noll, Carol Schwarz, Anne, Bob and Bryce St. Clair, Sheryl, Steve, Dad, Ray and Ruth, Ron and Barbara – Shane would arrive back in Flower Mound and come to Wichita Monday morning.

Jason and Steve took me to Lakeview to begin the plans which were finalized after Shane arrived on Monday and a return visit to Lakeview. Obituary notice prepared for Monday announcing services pending.

Food and calls and people continued until late evening. Jason stayed over again but exhaustion helped turn night into the next day.

March 25 – Monday

Steve and Sheryl helped keep lists of calls, visitors, and food.

Bay Hong had spoken to Roy working hard in the front yard. "Roy sad, no happy, always happy. He always talk to Bay – not Saturday – he only wave. It was 2:40." Bay went in to rest. Roy finished the front yard and mowed around to the back. He finished about once around the yard. Bay continued, "I got up to put a clean shirt to go get wife. She work. I look at watch it 3 p.m. I put shirt on. I no hear mower."

It would appear that Roy stopped, sat down by the fence and slumped over. When I found him, he still had on his hat, cell phone, radio earphones in his ears and face mask in place to protect from breathing dust. He essentially looked as if he had fallen asleep after sitting down to rest.

Shane arrived from Dallas at 1:30 p.m. Shane, Jason and I had an appointment at Lakeview Funeral Home at 3 p.m. Dad came too.

Decisions were made rather easy because we knew what Roy wanted, "a pine box buried in the back yard." We laughed at this silly memory.

Roy's body was ready by 5 p.m. and the three of us were led to the viewing room. We cried and cried and the shock of seeing him dead was like freezing rain on hearts warm with love.

March 26 – Tuesday

A trip to Lakeview, the Cessna Employees' Club Credit Union and on to Ruth and Ray's for dinner and a meeting with Pastor Dennis to share our memories and stories, tears and laughs.

Robert, Russell, and Marcel came from Washington and Oregon. Shelley arrived needing to leave Derek and Abby in Texas with her mother, Dot. Derek was sick and Abby not feeling well. They sent drawings to me. Derek had asked Shane about Papa's soul. "Was it in heaven?" He knew I could come to Texas but not Papa ever again. Abby remembered Papa singing in church and that made her happy.

Krystine hugged me and told me it would be alright, "Don't be sad; Papa is in heaven." Baby Hannah at four months will have to be told about her Papa.

A memory table of Roy's life was a joy to put together with the boys. From 6 to 9 p.m. at Lakeview the whole family greeted many, many Cessna employees and friends, WSU fans, church and neighborhood folks.

The viewing room was full of flowers. Jason took many pictures to help save the memory of a comforting evening with so many sharing our shock and slow awareness that our nightmare was not a dream.

But God is so good! No two sprays of flowers – no two cards the same. Dozens of cards come each day.

March 27 – Wednesday

Over 500 people came to the service. The church balcony was full, many stood in the full sanctuary and some 50 or more listened downstairs from Fellowship Hall without hymn books or orders of worship. Roy's family plus most of the aunts, uncles and cousins still alive were there. My sister Sheryl's son, Chuck, with his wife, Morgan, and daughter, Ella, came from San Leandro. Ed and Michelle called several times from Las Vegas. My sister Barbara and Frank and their big family came. Brother Bill and Donna and family were there.

After prayer with close family in the little chapel we walked into this huge crowd of witnesses. Don and Shirley Beggs (he is president of WSU) told me later that people were even standing outside the church in order to be close.

Cessna officials, with retired vice-president, Paul Kalberer, speaking in the service, shared memories of Roy.

God is good. The day was sunny, warm and breezy and the long procession to Lakeview included some thirty cars.

March 28 – Thursday

Shelley returned to Texas to put Derek in the hospital. The phone never stopped ringing with Steve still handling the calls. Shane and Jason reviewed papers and made a list of questions to be answered by the time the death certificates arrive in a few weeks. Decisions were made about credit cards, removing the cable box and plans to meet with the financial adviser and attorney in a few weeks were discussed.

Dinner at Cactus Cantina to toast Roy with strawberry margaritas included Sheryl, Chuck, Morgan, Ella, Jason, Kristen, Krystine, and Hannah, Steve, and was hosted by Shane. Some of us then headed to Java Villa for coffee. The little impromptu band playing Celtic music ended a lively, lovely evening sharing more memories and plans.

God is good!

March 28 – Friday

Shane drove back to Texas at 7 a.m. Jason returned to work at 1 p.m. Chuck and Morgan and Ella stayed the day to help with phone calls and errands.

March 29 – Saturday

Everyone is gone. I am alone.

How Ya' Doin'?

The routine question of, "How are you?" rattles around in my head like a few marbles in an old tobacco tin. The noisy rattling bangs back, "How the hell do you think I am? Roy died!"

Am I going to make it? This is the question that ricochets like slowed bullets caught in an empty oil drum. Bang, rattle, bang! I'm doing okay. I'm getting along. Bang, rattle, bang! My God, it's been twenty-one months. I'm fine, I guess. No way. Bang, rattle, bang!

I wake and get up before dawn. The darkness hides my fear of facing another day alone. Bang, rattle, bang!

As quick as I can, I shower, make up my face and pull on clothes adding earrings and my watch before splashing on cologne. I take my insulin shot and swallow the first of four rounds of daily prescribed meds. With cell phone and car keys, I leave on automatic pilot. My Saturn backs out of the garage before 7:00 a.m. and heads over to Harry and Hillside. In five minutes, if I get stopped at the light, the car parks in front of Chicago Donuts just a half-mile from home.

Yogi has my 21-oz. cup of fresh brewed black coffee poured and is reaching to get me my just-made powdered sugar donut as I sit down at the counter on the fourth stool from the cash register. "How you doing this morning," he asks in his thick British-Indian accent.

I give this generous, sensitive man my best, throat-choked "okay" and spread open the daily *Wichita Eagle* being careful not to spill the coffee. If I can get the paper read, I can pretend to care about what's happening in the rest of the world.

I try to concentrate around the banging in my head until the habitual "how ya' doing?" exchanges begin with the regulars. Wayne, Connie, Glenn, Fernando, Louise, Chief, and others without names are social interactions all self-help resources tell me are necessary to get through grief. Bang, rattle, bang!

Our laughter and joking gives testimony to my doing okay and the marbles rolling around in my head could be saying, "You are doing OK!" Bang, rattle, bang?

It is true – I don't cry as much. Bang, rattle, bang! But lumps in my throat still catch me off guard.

I survived the second round of Thanksgiving and Christmas and all those other holidays and anniversaries. Even enjoyed the bulging days of food, family and friends. Funny, but I found myself panicked for some peace and quiet before everyone headed back home. After they were all gone the old feelings of a house too big, too empty, and too quiet were noisy once again. Rattle, bang, rattle….

Symbols of Roy's presence are no longer abundant. Butterfly is now a password as I try to master Microsoft software for tracking daily business. It is time, again, for New Year's resolutions. Time to set some goals for the new me. Rattle, bang, rattle.

As the temperature dips to Kansas January lows, I find comfort in knowing a blanket of evergreens warms the ground where Roy is buried. My shoulders shiver with longing as I remember his strong, warm hugs. Rattle, bang, rattle.

The feel good of getting through each day is tempered by the still heavy weight of loss and aloneness.

※

Gene Blake reflects

"How ya' doin'?"
"Just fine."

Too often this common social interchange is simply an insincere inquiry followed by a false response. This is particularly true if one is grieving the death of a loved one or suffering from any significant loss. Our temptation usually is to respond in one of two ways. "Spilling our guts" by telling the other more than they want, or are prepared, to hear or, "Putting up a good front" – basically, lying about how well we are doing.

For several years I'd been on disability because of an undiagnosed condition related to my diabetes. For about six days each month I could neither function mentally or physically and spent most of my time in bed. After resigning from a full time pastorate I chose to serve a small church part time. It was about all I could handle. During this time I frequently encountered the greeting "How ya' doin'?"

One day I stopped by a friend's office to extend my condolences upon his son's suicide. Bob and his wife both had struggled with cancer and now faced this tragic loss. In the course of our conversation, he raised this question, "What do you say when people ask, 'How are you doing?'" We agreed some people are sincerely interested and concerned. For others it's the equivalent of saying, "Hello." Sometimes we know which is which, sometimes we don't. If we say, "Just fine," the first group will know we are lying and feel rebuffed. If we unload on the other group they will probably cross the street the next time they see us coming. I allowed Bob to talk about his quandary.

As he suspected, I'd dealt with the same issue. "How I've found myself responding," I said, "is to inject a little humor while giving the person an opportunity to delve deeper into my situation if they choose." I shared some of my favorite responses to: "How ya' doin'?"

- "My wife says I'm better than nothing – but not by much!"
- "I'm in good shape for an old man. If I were 95 I'd be great!"
- "Well, there're several schools of thought about that."
- "Fair to partly cloudy."
- "I'm up and around."

Invariably, the response is not superficial. Self-deprecating humor usually is well received. Often there's laughter followed by some verbal repartee. Sometimes the conversation takes a more serious turn. Whatever the response, it's the choice of the other person – not mine.

For instance, one afternoon I was walking past the bank as the receptionist was locking the front doors. "Hi, Gene," she greeted me, "How ya' doin'?"

"I'm in pretty good shape for an old man," I responded, "How 'bout you?"

"Well, I'm in good shape for a pregnant woman!"

Our conversation left the superficial and took a deeper, more serious turn. I inquired about her due date and asked, "Is this your first?" – questions about her obvious condition I never would have asked in casual conversation. We talked for some time about marriage, remarriage, and parenting. Most significantly, our relationship went from casual acquaintance to friendship – something that never would have happened if my, or her, initial response had been: "Fine."

How we respond to this casual greeting is our choice. Much of the time our response is equally casual. However, after losing a loved one, receiving a dreaded medical diagnosis, or any other traumatic loss, the apparent inquiry suddenly elicits a different reaction from us. We're not sure how to respond. We're not comfortable with lying nor are we sure the other person wants to know how much we're hurting. Definitely, we don't want to offend the sincere concern of a friend.

For some, injecting a little humor and allowing the other person to inquire further is workable. For others, this approach would seem totally foreign and inappropriate. But, however we choose to respond, it's important to allow the opportunity for those who are sincerely concerned to extend their comfort and care. ❋

Ebb and Flow

The feeling strengthens as the day begins to exit. I am tired of pretending to be happy. The desire to escape the dull existence and boring routine of living alone whispers to me like an invisible suitor. I push it aside but I really just want to run away from everything. I want to pack a bag and head for Hawaii.

Being seduced to use sleep as my escape makes no sense. It is the bedroom and bath where daily rituals of husband and wife routines are the strongest. Going to bed to sleep alone each night is the constant reminder that I am a widow. Even though the Old Spice deodorant-Noxzema shave cream-Avon cologne smell of Roy is long gone I am wedded to my bedtime routine. Makeup is creamed off. Jewelry placed in a dish that covers the water stain on the dresser left by his Diet Rite jug. Nightgown, left dumped down on the bed this morning, is rumpled comfort ready to cover my naked loneliness. Before nine I am sleepy but make myself wait until after the ten o'clock news report before giving in to the rest of my bedtime routine.

Bedtime meds include an injection of Lantus, my long-acting insulin. As I twist to reach my buttocks I remember how Roy would squeeze and tease me whenever he helped with my insulin shots. He could reach the unreachable places when abdomen or thighs were bruised. I swallow my last 100-mg. tablet of calcium-D with a glass of water. I make one more bathroom stop taking time to brush and floss then crawl in bed. Sleep overcomes my aloneness.

Once into bed I move Roy's pillow to lay lengthwise in the middle alongside of me. I pull it close. I smooth the cold pillowcase. I close my eyes and I feel his shoulder and back. When I pull the pillow tight, I feel my arm around his middle. It makes me feel secure.

My fingers make soft, silent pats on imagined shoulders – a goodnight habit of almost 39 years. Pat, pat, pat – quiet caresses in a rhythm that slows my breathing. I am warm. The reality of his death fades. I drift like a raft on a quiet sea.

The rhythm of this nighttime routine is like an ocean tide. The moon pulls up the water to blanket the beach. The collection of human debris left behind at low tide is covered once again with the incoming ocean making it easy to believe the beach is not cluttered with life's leftovers.

Before dawn I awaken to the cold reality that it has been almost two years since Roy's sudden, unexpected death. My respite retreats. The ebb tide reveals questions I left from the day before:

When will I feel the energy for living once again?

Will I ever live alone without being lonely?

How will I find a new identity? What do I want to do?

The questions flood me like tidal waves.

The slow, hard work of dealing with Roy's death is like the overwhelming task of cleaning up the shoreline torn apart by the hurricane raging of willful wind and wicked waves.

As the brittle cold of winter day is covered over by the star-sprinkled ebony blackness of winter night, feeling close to the one I will always love warms me. I am thankful sleep rests me and renews my strength to keep working at making this new life. I wake to await the longer light of upcoming spring.

Gene Blake reflects

It's tempting – especially for grief counselors – to divide the grieving process into stages. In the case of a sudden, unexpected death, one first encounters "shock" – a time when reality fails to penetrate our existence. Just as our bodies go into shock as a result of physical trauma, our emotions and mind enter a stage of shock to protect us from the dreaded reality of a loved one's death. In the case of a slow, lingering death one may first experience a sense of release. But, because the death of someone dear is such a basic change in our life, shock – though diminished – is still present. This stage of involuntary denial slowly gives way to the process of dealing with our loss.

While coming to grips with our new situation we may visit those places where we feel closer to the deceased: their grave, a particular chair, their side of the bed. Our imaginations bargain with our reality. Ever so slowly we let go of the one who has been an integral part of our lives.

As we look back over our grieving process we may glimpse how we've lived through the defined stages. But we also become aware of the ebb and flow – the going back and forth through the stages, retracing our steps. The death of a close friend or relative – or other traumatic experience – can put us back to square one. We may not stay there as long but all the feelings of vulnerability and insecurity are again real. The stages are there, but they are fluid – they ebb and flow. On a good day we may see our progress, but on a bad day we may feel like we're falling back.

Society gives us one or two weeks for a grieving process that takes an equivalent number of years – not that we ever get over the death of a loved one, but we slowly come to accept our new life. The processes of learning to cope with a new reality and developing a new identity leave us feeling uncertain, impatient, and frustrated. But, for most, there comes a day when we realize we've grown as a person. We're wiser, more understanding of others, less superficial, and more appreciative of every day. Some even become aware they are empowered to assist others in their grieving process.

One Step

The first time I prayed to God after Roy's death was a body prayer. I could clasp my hands in prayer and stretch my arms outward following a familiar pattern I first learned at a Presbyterian Women in the Synod of Mid-America meeting. But I could not speak the words. To pray to the God who could take away my beloved husband just because another angel in heaven was needed was asking too much of my sob-choked throat.

I could raise my arms in thanksgiving for the sky above my head and stoop low in thankfulness for the earth beneath my feet. But my dry mouth would not allow even words of lament to escape my wounded soul to be heard by the ears of God.

Outstretched arms would express a glory for the world all around me but trying to say the words strangled me.

Stepping forward, putting one foot in front of the other was visible witness to a promise to step out on faith that my mind could not comprehend nor my heart commit to.

My arms reached to encircle my weak shoulders as a promise to take care of myself. Tears dripped to the floor as my hands made soft pats on my lonely shoulders.

Standing to reach again towards heaven to express thanksgiving for a new day was made possible only by God reaching down to lift me up. My body felt old, broken, drained of almost all of my life.

Thirty-nine years of my almost fifty-nine years had evaporated from my physical self as the growing reality of Roy's death so sudden, so unexpected, and too soon became my routine waking first thoughts.

Standing in the dark before first light, facing east at my three-by-four-foot curtain-less kitchen window I presented myself to God and moved my body through these motions of unspoken prayer. It was for me a mantra to help me face reality. But the silent movement was like a fleshless bone. A bare attempt to pray. The daily ritual was my goal until a time would come when praying words could form again in my heart and escape my lips to praise God and speak my need.

With one step at a time, putting one foot in front of the other, stretching up, bending low, and reaching out I was able to continue my grief journey.

The second anniversary of Roy's dying is but three days away. I have begun to love the colors of the landscape again. I feel refreshment in the wave of wind-filled tree limbs pregnant with promise. My ears hear singing birds seeking partners for their own ventures of nesting. It is ritual. It is faith. It transforms.

What Comes Next?

"The future belongs to those who believe in the beauty of their dreams."
Eleanor Roosevelt, 1884-1962

Urge is a good word. My *American Heritage Dictionary* defines this verb as meaning to drive forward or onward forcefully. Used in a sentence, I feel the urge to be back in charge of my life. Grief has been in control. I think I am getting strong enough to act – not just react.

I am one of the lucky widows. I have many options and resources available to me. One could say the "sky is the limit."

But I want to stay grounded. I want to stay close to the earth. I don't want to start doing foolish things and worry my kids. I don't have the urge to go looking for a man to rescue me from the hard work of living without a life partner.

Taking control of my life is to figure out what I want and what I don't want. To believe there are options. Maybe set some priorities. To make lists again of what I want to do not just lists of what I have to do. To schedule on the calendar some fun things.

Make decisions, even temporary ones. Stay in my home for at least five years? Consider alternative housing – buy a duplex, condominium or patio home? If I make a commitment to continue living here in this too big house for at least five years, then my options become more of a to-do list – clean the rain gutters, replace the kitchen floor, keep the heating and air conditioning in good condition, sort out the stored stuff in the garage and closets.

And the yards – front and back. Hired help has mowed and trimmed these first two summers. A watering system of some sort has been flooding my mind. But is the expense or even trouble worth it?

Should I be concerned about the neighborhood's changing value and just what change might that be? Or is there a growing risk regarding rising crime? Will I continue to feel safe? No easy answers. I feel like I have muddied the waters, again. But I have to figure out the questions before I can make things happen.

This is how I will begin.

Meet with Mary the real estate lady to talk about this house and take a look at other options. Talk with a landscaper about at least some changes. Roy and I were ready to do this the year he died. On the first anniversary of his death I wrote about the future and said, "I can landscape with boulders and butterfly bushes." I can start there.

I have already checked out the loan company to get the current interest rate available on my home equity account. Four-and-one-half percent is pretty good right now.

When I talked to John, my financial adviser, he told me I could do anything I want – the sky's the limit kind of talk. No blank check but he gave me good advice – check out all possibilities, be patient and trust my instincts.

As I sit here in front of my laptop, Roy's picture appears on my screen saver. I think he might be saying, "You do what you want to do. But if you had died first I would choose to stay in our home."

This is the difference. I am now able to say "my" home. Cleaning out drawers, closets, and files can wait for today. I want to check the yellow pages for a landscaper.

Red Roses

Three long stem yellow roses, that's all I want. It is 10 a.m. and Tillie's Floral has lily white, baby-cheeks pink, and red, but no yellow long stem or short stem roses. I sigh my disappointment. One clerk is taking an order by phone and two others are waiting on customers ahead of me.

A five-foot-ten and trim 20-something male wearing khaki slacks and a short-sleeve plain white cotton polo-type casual shirt selects a dozen of the baby pink roses. The clerk adds two sprigs of tiny white Baby's Breath as she wraps them in green tissue paper. I picture in his nervous face and my imagination the flowers will accompany a small diamond engagement ring and a marriage proposal over lunch. How lucky, I thought.

My turn now and I pick the blood red, velvety roses with short stems. Short meaning sixteen inches long. They have the look of royalty and are open just beyond the tight bud stage.

I say "no" to Baby's Breath and "yes" to leafy green fern. Linn wraps the red dozen in green tissue paper and ties a simple bow around the bouquet with a red satin ribbon half-an-inch wide. The satin ends hang down and look like two streams of blood flowing from a broken heart. Two ribbons of tears escape my eyes and make wet rivulets down each side of my nose. My lips curve up in a smile of apology but I can't see Linn's face. I grope for a Kleenex in my bulging tote bag.

Today is the third wedding anniversary day, June 15, since Roy died. So I just need three roses for Roy's grave but on Tuesdays at Tillie's the roses are "cheaper by the dozen." I tell myself it is okay for me to keep and enjoy the remaining nine.

Back home and in a hurry, I leave three velvet roses in the green tissue wrapping and put nine gorgeous rose buds into a keepsake clear glass vase saved from his funeral. I run cold tap water stirring in the packet of fresh flower preservative. Much to my surprise one tight bud tucked deep into the middle of the bouquet is not the rich red velvet of the others but is instead a barely open bud of burnt-orange suede. Wow! It is a sign, a symbol. Of what, I do not know.

Thirty minutes later I am standing at the foot of Roy's grave. I apologize for royal red instead of our wedding bouquet yellow and the salty tears of grief flow down my cheeks and drip to the rain damp ground.

The yellow rose bouquets Roy gave me almost every year for our wedding anniversary are 35mm snapshots moving page by page in the album of my mind. The last one was waiting for us at the Old Town Hotel nine months before he died and the large, round, gold vase held 38 deep golden yellow roses. His secret conspiracy with Tillie's and the hotel manager to surprise me was a smile with hugs and kisses success.

Three blood-red royal velvet roses on this third wedding anniversary date after his death pale in comparison. And more tears drip to the rain damp ground.

Gene Blake reflects

After you do something three times, it becomes a tradition. I coined this saying while serving as a Presbyterian pastor. Of course, I was thinking in terms of a special service, program, or dinner. The truth of this axiom quickly became obvious when someone suggested we dispense with some now popular, if new, tradition. The mere mention could raise the hackles of both young and old. It's as much our human nature to create traditions as it is to resist change.

The role of tradition and ritual in our lives is often underestimated. Trimming the Christmas tree, exchanging gifts, preparing holiday meals, celebrating birthdays and anniversaries, all of these bring a continuity and expectation to our lives that transcends age. Traditions are to couples and families what habits are to individuals. They provide a degree of certainty and comfort while nurturing memories and creating stories.

Imagine what it would be like to brush your teeth if the process wasn't a habit. You'd have to consider each step: unscrewing the cap, squeezing the tube just right, brushing up, brushing down, etc. Likewise, when a loved one dies, we have to reorient our lives, change old habits, part with some beloved traditions, and create new ones. We're surprised at how frustrated and angry we can become, how quickly tears well up, and how we search for signs of hope.

The loss of a loved one steals cherished traditions and robs us of an expected future. We feel lost, violated, and insecure. We struggle to reestablish some semblance of order and continuity to our existence – some vision of what lies ahead. Suddenly, hope and trust are less an abstract desire, but instead, become a more concrete need as we walk into a foreign future.

One author put it this way: "Trust allows us to dance on the edge of what is, while trusting in a tomorrow we cannot see. Trust is not being sure where you're going anyway – like embracing a journey without a map. Sometimes trust is better understood as a verb than a noun."

I'm reminded of a comment uttered many times by an elderly couple before their deaths: "Things will work out." I've often referred to it as a statement of faith, but it also exemplifies trust – trust that things will work out even if one can't conceive of how that might happen. Or, as I've also heard it put, "Show up, tell the truth, detach from the outcome, and do what is before you today." ✾

Waiting

*"The most beautiful stones have been tossed by the wind
and washed by the waters and polished to brilliance
by life's strongest storms."*
Author Unknown

"Waiting, for what?" you might ask and so do I. The weather to clear? My energy level to increase? A bright idea to pop into my mind?

I am waiting for things over which I have no control. Things like the legal action pending on my dad's last will and testament filed by his not quite ex-wife. I have been waiting a year on her family, her health, her attorneys and mine, and the courts. This waiting is like being held hostage in a bank holdup. I am tied hand and foot and the robbers are hooded. They hold an Uzi machine gun to my head.

I am waiting for the new landscape project for my home to be completed. Since Roy died the lawn's only been mowed and edged week after week.

The backyard has new trees and shrubs already planted to soften the harshness of the memory of the place where Roy died. But the new back porch is waiting for one more limestone slab step and the air conditioner has not been moved and reconnected. It will be 80 degrees again today. The light rain this morning has kept the crew somewhere else and the boss does not return from Las Vegas until tomorrow.

The front yard still has a front-loader parked in it and the driveway is storage for several tons of sandstone to lay a footpath and outline for the raised beds. More trees and bedding plants have yet to arrive while soil is still to being prepared.

Is it the weather or the landscapers making me wait?

I want to mark this project off my list. I am ready to write the check to pay off the balance. I am ready to start making payments on the loan. I want to have coffee on my new porch and watch the sunrise in the east. I am ready for color-filled surroundings, and peace, and a new project.

I am eager to cross something off my list that is more than "pick up prescriptions at Osco." I want to have the energy and free time to devote to Shane and Derek and Abby when they come on June 26. I don't want them to have to walk in mud.

I want some closure on the last year of my dad's life and his death last August. I want to be through with going through his house and things again. I don't want to call attorneys for the latest updates and I don't want to worry about his estranged wife's family.

I must take a deep breath and keep walking on down this road. I want the road to go somewhere. Is that possible? Will it ever happen?

I have to keep walking even while I wait.

Gene Blake reflects

"The only thing I hate worse than waiting on someone is having someone wait on me!" I don't know how many times I've uttered these words. I'm not good at waiting. When I was young, I couldn't wait to grow up. I always wanted to be older: old enough to operate a tractor, to work on a ranch, to drive a car, to be through school and college, to get out into the workplace. Now I'm older, wiser, and somewhat more patient. I can wait to die.

Years ago I took a Myers-Briggs Personality Inventory test. This instrument rates a person in four categories – the last category measures one's inclination to either quickly bring a situation to closure or to string things out indefinitely. Myers-Briggs correctly gauged my tendency to be impatient and to get things done. I suspect those who share this trait and who have lost a loved one have more difficulty dealing with grief than those who don't. The grieving process takes time – lots of time, often more time than we or the society around us are inclined to allow.

It's also quite typical for a second loss to interrupt our grieving process. If another family member or good friend dies we feel as if we're "back to square one" in dealing with the initial loss. We become even more impatient and discouraged because we no longer see any progress. This setback is frustrating; however, it usually is temporary.

In the midst of grieving, we find we are less able to deal with stress, disappointment, and frustration. Friends and family members may accuse us of developing a "short fuse." Anger and impatience are near the surface of our feelings. It's difficult to accept our emotions as normal for a grieving person.

It's a very human tendency to attempt to control our lives – to plan, to prepare, and to avoid unnecessary risk. But our ability to do so is limited. Untimely illness, death, an accident, or another tragedy can foil our best laid plans and expectations. Only the suicidal plan their deaths, and only the aged and those deemed "terminal" have ample warning.

Often death comes as a shock to a person's family. For instance, a person dying of cancer has the opportunity to get their affairs in order, say their goodbyes, and to prepare for death mentally and spiritually. Loved ones have some of the same opportunities. However, they have to watch a person slowly decline – often in discomfort or pain. Caring for a loved one in these circumstances can be a very heavy burden.

On the other hand, someone who dies quickly and unexpectedly may not suffer as much, but neither is there the opportunity to prepare. And, the reaction of loved ones is shock – shock that can last for weeks. Suddenly their lives are in turmoil – a turmoil that seemingly lasts for an eternity.

However we experience the death of a loved one, we wait,
- wait for an understanding of what we've experienced,
- wait for hope,
- wait for a new identity,
- wait for life to return to some degree of normalcy,
- wait for an uncertain future. ❦

It's About Time

Courage doesn't always roar. Sometimes courage is the quiet voice at the end of the day saying, "I will try again tomorrow."
Anonymous

They said it would take time.
They were right.
Some said the second year is harder.
They were right.
After two years and almost four months time seems to fly.
But that's wrong.
It is an eternity. It is fast forward but agonizing and pain-filled.
It seems to have no end.
They said it would begin to be better.
They were right.
Several said it takes years.
They were right.
After two years and almost four months time seems to stand still.
And it has.
It is an eternity.
It is slow motion.
It is stretching and strengthening.

Krystine and Three Trees

"Krystine keeps worrying about her Papa, crying a lot – even at Chad and Deanna's wedding. She says she just misses him." Jason spoke with quiet concern as any dad would. He went on, "It has been almost three years since Dad died and Kristen and I decided to take her to Three Trees, a non-profit organization that provides support and comfort for grieving children and their families. We wonder if you would like to go with us."

"Of course I'll go. I think you're wise to find some help for her and yourselves. I've wondered from the beginning how everyone would deal with your dad's death especially the children. You know how much the sharing with others in Good Grief meetings helped me."

Jason went on to explain some things that have been happening. Krystine prays for Papa at bedtime and says it helps her have good dreams about him. But she wakes up crying. The dreams are about the fun things they use to do – flying in the airplane and Papa massaging her feet. "Krystine says it makes her miss Papa more. Sometimes she gets out of control and cries pretty hard. It is happening more often."

A couple of hours every Monday evening for seven weeks Krystine met in a group of children her own age who were also missing loved ones – most had lost a parent. While Jason and Kristen met with other parents who had brought children I met in yet another small group. They all had two things in common – bewildered children with heartbreaking losses and a need to learn how to cope with their own grief.

I was startled to see so many young mothers whose husbands were dead. One father's two young sons were acting out at school and even bullying each other. Another shared how her teenage son had withdrawn from his friends and was failing in school after his dad's motorcycle accident.

Krystine began to talk about her good dreams about airplane rides with Papa. Dreams hiding in Papa's clothes closet waiting to scare him when he changed clothes after getting home from work. He soon caught on and would scare her with a "boo" first when he opened the closet door. Startled screams would be followed by belly-clutching laughter. Krystine's eyes get weepy as her quiet voice shares her loss.

Krystine tells me she learned at Three Trees that it is okay to cry when you miss somebody. "We made a vase from a flower pot and colored markers. We wrote our name and things we liked on a note. I didn't want to keep it. I wanted to put it on Papa's grave because it was like when I made him birthday cards and Christmas presents. I drew lots and lots and lots of pictures of me and Papa and Jesus. I know Jesus is going to take care of him in heaven because we are family. I got a blanket at Three Trees to keep and hold close when I remember.

And we let go of balloons to watch them fly up into the sky. I think of Papa jumping from cloud to cloud to catch mine. I keep this magazine because it has an ad about Three Trees and I see ads in different places like once in a restroom at a restaurant. I am always happy when I see something about Three Trees. I might go there again sometime."

The Next Days

The invitation to travel with Gene Blake was prompted, as always, by his concern for driving alone and having one of his episodes that leaves him unable to drive.

Leaving home on March 24th for this trip reminds me of my first trip away from the house after Roy died. To leave and return home is not so hard now.

Gene and I are considering collaborating on a book. My stories share the personal experiences and his stories reflect on them to give support using his counselor, pastoral, academic experience. Gene's work as a facilitator for grief and divorce support groups makes him a helpful resource for learning to grieve well.

I continue to write because things keep happening. The highs and lows of living day to day are like a roller coaster. Getting together a couple of times a month with some women like me for dinner or a play has added a social dimension that is proving helpful. We have the common bond of the death of our husbands but we hate the word "widow." Because we are still having ups and downs we call ourselves the Yo-Yos.

Lots of good things are happening. My writing has helped me know Roy better. I even know myself better. These revelations are healing.

Thinking back is like watching those old 8mm home movies we made when the boys were young. We matured through the years, which is more obvious when I see how much hair Roy had in the 1970s and how skinny we both were. Our busy family life slowing into pre-retirement fun as our years together added up. Bell bottom pants were in and out and back in style as time passed. I love how often we wore the same old shirts made comfortable and soft from washing after washing.

I still have pictures and some personal files to go through. But his side of the clothes closet is empty. The middle drawer in the bedroom dresser where he deposited the contents of his pockets each night is still full of keys, combs, ID cards, pens, watches and billfold.

A small covered basket made from palm tree fronds that I brought back from Hawaii on a Shocker baseball trip gives me a special place to fill with other keepsakes that were so much a part of him. Like the small square pill case that held eight Mylanta tablets stacked in two layers. He carried it for years when indigestion was a regular after meal event. But ten years ago, for some reason, those episodes of burp disappeared. I found the pill case in the hall along with an almost empty bottle of green extra strength Mylanta tablets. I know it is not crazy to hang on to these things.

Derek voiced a wish to have Papa's watch and his jug – the Coleman quart insulated drinking mug that Roy always filled with Diet Rite cola.

My next days have no need to be wasted. I want to get some things out of the way in order to feel free to have fun with my family and make new friends. But waste days I will – for this I am sure. Transition is very hard work and it takes time.

To seek joy in these tasks, to be happy and busy are my goals.

An outbreak of allergy symptoms has me feeling punk. I am ready to "waste" a few days in Texas, then get the landscaping done and some old limestone boulders planted. I want to go to Hawaii next year with the Shockers and there are WSU baseball games this weekend. There is still that darned Microsoft Money to master.

The sweeper, dust rags, empty boxes, air freshener, and Pine-Sol seem content to wait. I love planning for the next days.

Life Lessons From the Landscape

> *"Then God commanded, 'Let the earth produce all kinds of plants, those that bear grain and those that bear fruit' – and it was done. So the earth produced all kinds of plants, and God was pleased by what God saw."*
> Genesis 1:11 and 12

While walking through my new garden/yard with the landscape designer I am intent on learning the names of new shrubs, trees and perennials. Long narrow green and white striped leafed drapes are liriope. They have spire-like stems coated with purple bulb-shaped flowers about the size of kitchen match heads. Butterfly bushes have small green, silver undercoated leaves. The teeny blossoms extend into purple swoops that cup the nectar, which intoxicates their namesake. Silver green lamb's ears, shaped like its name, is soft to touch. Long and wide, supple dark brown ovals growing along long limbs look like their name too – leather leaf viburnum. Planted in the shady dark corner right outside the window where I write, it will grow to the rooftop.

    A scrumptious maroon-leafed Canadian cherry tree stands sentry to tart Limemound spirea and pale citrus green-leafed mock orange. The pink cotton candy-colored creeping roses are planted to sweeten a path to the rustic birdbath. The surrounding watermelon-colored roses brighten a place of honor and memory to Roy. Six rose-of-sharon shrubs with pink hibiscus-sized flowers guard the perimeter to the south.

    This place in the backyard landscape is meant to celebrate Roy's life, not commemorate the place where he died. His chain-link bordered yard of perfect Bermuda grass was testimony to his responsible nature. Mowed and watered religiously from early spring until late fall Roy's pride was edged and trimmed to be as neat as his desk at Cessna Aircraft Company. The lush wall of elderberry bushes growing to an unusual height of seven feet along the south fence were the only frills of flowers in that yard. Canopies of tiny white blossoms larger than the span of Roy's outstretched hand turned into small black purple berries for the birds to pick bare.

The landscaper brings me back to the present and begins to instruct me in the tending of this low-maintenance extravagance I call Eden. The tending-to is one of the objectives needed to carry out this first long-term goal written on my life plan for a future without my Bermuda grass-loving husband.

The wide new flower beds, free flowing around the yard and house, are testimony to my liquid personality. The outcrops of limestone boulders hauled from a quarry near Winfield, Kansas, with the help of my long-time friend, Gene Blake, anchor this colorful dream come true.

Pointing to my personal favorites, the eleven clumps of daylilies called Stella de Oro, the landscaper reminds me that I must wait until the flower stems are brown and pull up easy from the ground before I remove them. I have to wait until the blossoms shrivel before snapping them off. It takes some time for all of the nutrients from green stems and leaves and golden flowers to re-enter the soil. Then, and only then, is the life cycle complete. By waiting I allow the plan to work. It is a design that provides sustenance for the next growing generation of beauty and joy in order to flourish in its calling and give testimony to life in all of its fullness.

This lesson is patience.

And if seeds appear before time to pull up the released stems, I must pick them and scatter them about on the ground. Leaving them attached is a signal to the plant that the season has come to an end. I want the plants to keep blooming throughout the spring, summer and into fall. I want them to trumpet loud the comfort they give me and to stand strong in my new garden in order to embolden me throughout the shorter days and longer nights of winter. The beauty of the Stella de Oro is the picture of transforming life growing into the future.

Throughout its days the Stella grows where it is planted, drawing strength from the soil. Water, sun and dark of night contribute to the symbiosis needed to nurture sturdy roots, steady the plant and bring bud to blossom in full color.

I grow where I am planted. I rediscover a solid foundation in the symbiosis of family, especially my sisters, Sheryl and Barbara, and in friendships that have held fast, and communities of faith and neighborhood.

I find strength in new people, new challenges, in anticipation, and in waiting. When I am tired, I can rest on my back porch sitting in an old, once-painted-white, red metal lawn chair bought from a junk dealer.

The lesson is that life does not end with the fading of flower or even the pulling up of dry brown stem no longer clinging steadfast to root. The lesson is that life does not end with our dying. Life is cycle not circle. Life is transforming. Living in relationship nurtures and sustains the next generation of beauty and joy in the garden so lovingly planted by the Landscaper "in the beginning."

Gene Blake reflects

What can we learn from the natural world around us – the grass, flowers, trees, and shrubs? What are the "life lessons" they teach us?

Plants and people need to be nurtured. As grass needs water to flourish in a scorching Kansas summer, we humans need the "living water" of a spiritual life to keep us grounded as we face the struggles of life – particularly the grieving process. Sherry's faith has been a vital source of hope as she looked to an unplanned, uncertain future.

Plants are more patient than people. It takes time for a seed to sprout, a plant to grow, a blossom to appear. I find it difficult to wait for sweet corn, planted in April, to provide a good meal in July. I want to hurry it up. Sherry, however, has demonstrated wisdom in not hurrying the grieving process, but giving herself the much needed time to heal. The flowers and fruits in our garden tell us to be patient. Good grieving, like a good harvest, takes time.

Plants and people can be co-creators of beauty. Roy died in their backyard. Sherry could have left the area to grow up in weeds, uncut grass, and overgrown trees. Instead, she chose to create a beautiful space as a memorial to Roy, establishing a place of solace, peace, and comfort.

Both plants and people have their cycles. In the spring, trees have buds that slowly swell before breaking forth into leaves – leaves that slowly grow in summer to their full size as the trunk of the tree adds an annual ring. In fall, those leaves turn varying shades of yellow, red, and brown, providing a new beauty. In winter they depart the nurturing branches with the help of an arctic blast of wind. In a similar fashion, a pregnant woman's abdomen swells before a baby is thrust into a new world. In a life span, not unlike a tree's, that baby grows into a child, an adolescent, and an adult, eventually to depart into another existence. Just as a tree leaves behind seeds and shoots, we humans leave behind families to start the cycle once again. I've admired the way Sherry has more fully opened her life to her family and others around her.

Plants and people often need to be pruned. My master gardener wife frequently works until dark on a summer's evening doing something she calls "deadheading." After roses or phlox have bloomed she nips off the old blossoms so the plant will bloom again. In the spring, she also cuts back our black raspberry bushes so they will produce more and larger fruit. It has not been easy for me learn these pruning lessons. Nor is it easy for most people to realize they can grow and become more fruitful as the result of the losses in their life. I feel Sherry has learned this most difficult of life's lessons.

Plants and people die, but the rocks remain. They remind us of eternity. Created millions of years ago, they will, no doubt, still remain millions of years from now. Yet we transient plants and people survive because of our transforming life cycles.

I've heard the phrase: "descend into our grief." What a perceptive description of the emotions we experience following the death of a loved one. It is tempting to resist the descent – to try to deny or suppress those terrible feelings and get on with our lives – to live in a perpetual summer. Yet the landscape of fall and winter teach us that life is on hold for a time before again breaking forth like trees and flowers in spring. As the winter of our grief loses its grip, our spirits ascend as does the sap in trees with the arrival of spring. We begin to heal and are better prepared for the difficult decisions concerning our identity and the future. Rooted in her faith, Sherry is now more at peace with her situation having learned life lessons from the landscapes that surround her. ✤

Finding Peace: Another Lesson

It is the rain that causes me to pause at my window here in my cabin called Willow No. Four. This free space of time is always on the schedule for Writing Festival Week.

My hope was to get out in the cool of October warmed with gleaming sun to stretch my spirit and explore Ghost Ranch. Last year a dry creek crossover behind the staff house led to this mysterious mound with honed, square, tile-like rocks left in piles like factory rejects. More exploration was my intention for free time today.

Drenched hope is a good reason to follow Ina's assignment and write about anything I want. After editing yesterday's work I take a break from my computer screen to soak up the view.

The landscape unfolds before me like my life has these past few years. Right out my window in Willow is a rocking chair. I wish I would take time to sit in it, drinking hot coffee and watching the dark of five a.m. disappear at the command of dawn.

Two steps from the empty rocking chair is a large log pole holding up the porch roof. This pole removes an 8-inch strip from the panorama of alfalfa field, open ground, golden-leaf cottonwoods with trunks and limbs that look like black oil paint on canvas. The trees color and interrupt the view of low-level, multi-layered cliffs painted gray in the rain and smudged with fog.

This whole rainy scene is interrupted by an appearance at the screened door by my friend, Gene. He comes in to invite me over to the dining hall for coffee. Having no need to think twice I grab two berry almond crispy snack bars, arm on my black and gold WSU Shocker jacket then pull on my brown corduroy hat to keep my ears warm.

On our boggy trek to the dining hall, we trample over fallen cottonwood leaves. They look like faded carpet in an old apartment.

In the dining hall, Kathy, looking for respite, joins us for her afternoon break from writing. Her cold, red nose had also been to the grindstone for two hours working on her next assignment for Ina. She sat down with us to commiserate.

Our conversation covers an encyclopedia of topics as we watch the fog lift off the mountains to the southwest.

With free time slipping away like leather boots on a muddy road, Gene and I head back to our individual creative writing ventures.

The sky retrieves its blue as the forecasted front follows its predictable path through the valley. I watch the warm, growing glow of late afternoon lift the cloudy veil from the mountains that have a powdered sugar coating of snow.

Again at my window, the gray color in the cliff face behind staff house has vanished. The spotlight of direct sunshine delineates the colors of ages of transformation. The wet green pine trees reach tall to impact and soften the massive stone testament to life eternal.

After supper the alfalfa becomes a Bed & Breakfast for deer to graze their fill and take safe refuge for the night. I thought their reservation was for a late arrival after dark. As I watch, a few of the deer watch back.

As this free day comes to a close, I look out my Willow window again. A black velvet cloth covers the sky with brilliant diamond-like stars arrayed in familiar patterns. These heavenly bodies give testimony to the endlessness of time as they pursue their eons-old trajectory. I am reminded of the Eskimo Legend found in one of my grief resources:

Perhaps
They are not
Stars in the sky,
But rather
Openings
Where our
Loved ones
Shine down to
Let us know
They are happy.

Some Things Never Change

I love
Books by Anonymous
Old books
Stories for children
Murder mysteries.
I love
Sunsets and sunrises reflecting off clouds
Saturn and Jupiter
Starry nights
A harvest moon.
I love
Baby smiles
Toddler's exploring
Old folks and teens killing time in the Mall
Time alone.
I love
Landscapes by Ansel Adams
Vincent Van Gogh's Sunflowers
Trees dressed in fall colors
A winter evergreen blanket for Roy's grave.
I love to eat
Things that crunch.
I love
Conversation
Odd words
Debate
Eye contact.
I love to drink
Coffee with a meal
Coffee after a meal
Coffee with donuts
Ruinite Lambrusco wine with shrimp scampi.
I love trying at least one new thing each year that I have never done before.
I love the routine of my new life.
I love to feel in control again.
I guess some things do change.

Treasure Island

It is early morning, New Year's Eve day, Shane's 41st birthday. I'm in the darkness of Abby's room with dawn just below the horizon. Before leaving my bed I do my routine set of leg stretches just because I am awake and it is too early to rise. With muscles warmed and my eyes focused it seems to be the perfect time to write on this last day of the year.

It is almost three years and I sometimes still feel like I am stumbling along on a moonless night. This dark I call the shadow of death can make even bright daylight feel like dusk on a cloudy day. In spite of all I have been able to do since March 23, 2002, I am still exploring my way.

My time of deep mourning has been wave after wave of unpredictable feelings and predictable experiences. This morning, after 365 times two plus nine months of days, the onslaught has ebbed. I am surviving a tidal wave of grief. Unlike tens of thousands of victims of the tsunami that followed the earthquake in the Indian Ocean on December 26th I am not dead but alive and even well.

At the end of any age, the new era has already had its beginning. I can say that I have felt like this before even though each night I go to bed thinking of Roy. To survive and not drown doesn't seem to mean much if you wake up washed ashore on a deserted island.

Or does it?

Tom Hanks, in his popular movie of a few years ago called, *Castaway*, found even a deserted island had resources for survival.

The television series called, *Survivor*, is a reality based depiction of how men and women, often on an island, find ways to do things that they have never done before. Their goal is to win the big prize with movie or TV screen crews standing in the wings ready to throw them a life line.

I am more than a survivor. My search has been for the ability to be happy living alone without being lonely. I have found buried treasures.

My goal to do at least one new thing each year that I have never done before has resulted in a submarine ride off the coast of Kona,

Hawaii, an Alaskan cruise along the inside passage, a pedicure, and even an honorable mention in a writing contest sponsored by *Byline Magazine* for *A Contemporary Psalm of Lament*.

Our family, each one overwhelmed in their own mourning, has been my life line. And my good friend, Gene Blake, continues to help me hike and chart a new life course. His quiet listening and wise sharing of experience have helped me understand what goes on during grief and I have gained confidence in myself. I have been able to stay sturdy and on course in the midst of a mighty storm.

I have found life again. Like treasure in a junk shop. A frameless watercolor canvas with spring-colored splashes. Gilded framed oil still life of berries in a basket. Landscapes of field, forest and stream. Portraits of children and grandfathers. As I explore, other delights stand stacked on and around an old white paint-chipped metal lawn chair. I bought the lawn chair for my back porch.

On this last day of another year, I turn to walk forward facing into the wind.

Happy New Year to Me – Chinese That Is!

Shane and family are putting Christmas stuff away. I take advantage of staying out of their way and write while sitting in Barnes and Noble. I spent Christmas morning with Jason and his family in Wichita and have been in Texas since December 26th.

At 6:30 p.m. on Christmas evening, my choices appeared to be either The Shanghai on East Harry in hometown Wichita, Kansas, or Denny's just across the street. The Chinese buffet was packed but Denny's lot was almost full as well. Either way I wouldn't be alone. Turning right into the mall and right again into the parking lot my impulse choice was The Shanghai. The buffet had more choices and better service but was more expensive. I was just glad to find something open on Christmas Day evening. It was Saturday. It was shivery cold and midnight dark, already.

But now at 12:50 p.m. on New Year's Day, I opt for lunch at the just-opened Panda Express. Located on the upper level of a shopping venue, the fast-food deli of Chinese entrées replaces a Schlotsky's Sandwich eatery. After making an easy left turn with a green arrow onto MacArthur Street from Highway 3040 I made another left to park across from the stairs leading up to the second level door front.

Sitting in the Panda Express I find myself stirring through a paper cup of steamy hot and sour soup looking for the last of the tofu and water chestnuts. There are unknown stringy vegetables that I choose to ignore floating in the spicy hot beef-brown broth. My preference is for egg drop soup but the hot and sour "soup of the day" is tasty. I fish out any egg the cook stirred into the hot broth. A chicken egg roll dipped in hot mustard rounds out my lunch.

Sitting by the window at a table for two I watch the busyness of folks out and about to post-Christmas shop and eat. It is an unusual 70 degree day in Flower Mound, Texas.

Now I notice the ten very large medicine ball-size red paper lanterns hanging over my head. Red is the color of good luck in China. Six eighteen-inch stems of bamboo stand tall in a gray clay jar decorating a table in the center of the eating space. Teeny red tassels hang from several arm-like limbs. These arms hold lots of unfolding green leaves and stretch up and out from the stalks. I can't remember the meanings but the numbers of things is also symbolic in Asian cultures. And bamboo brings good luck.

A sign reads Happy New Year. I ask a waitress, "When is the Chinese New Year?" She looks to other staff for a sign of knowing. They look back and shrug. In perfect English, the American-born Asian young lady says, "We know it is some time in February." I sigh with relief. I have time to get a card for the Hongs – my Wichita next door neighbors on South Estelle who came from Vietnam in 1997.

My fortune found on the small strip of paper pulled from the traditional after dinner cookie says, "Your independence shall lead you to bold adventure." I take that to mean, "Happy New Year to me"!

Gene Blake reflects

Loneliness versus independence: these are competing issues facing many who have been widowed for some time. On one hand, loneliness motivates us to start dating or at least consider that option. On the other hand, a newly-found independence may cause us to value our freedom – particularly when it's coupled with personal confidence.

These were alternatives expressed during a conversation in my office one day. Three women, all in their 40s ... two divorced, one widowed; two executives, one a professional person; all attractive and well respected in the community ... were discussing the pros and cons of dating and possible remarriage. They arrived at the consensus they were weighing their loneliness against a desire for independence. Two of the three eventually remarried.

Marriage is no more a guarantee of happiness than singleness. Since many second marriages occur when we've established our likes, dislikes, values, priorities, habits, and opinions, many compromises and changes are involved in a new relationship. A comment I've heard directly and indirectly several times from women is: "I don't want to train another husband." No doubt most men don't want to be retrained – even though they may not be totally aware of the process.

Yet many people have the desire for a little adventure in their lives – something new, different, exciting. Venturing into a new relationship can provide a bit of spark to our routine, giving us a reason to face an uncertain future with anticipation.

However, I also recall two bits of wisdom gleaned from the bereavement support groups I led: It's wise to re-establish your identity as a single person before considering remarriage. Granted, it's tempting to, in essence, go from one marriage into another without this change in identity, but it's not the smart thing to do. There is an accepted custom of waiting at least a year before remarrying out of respect for the deceased. It's an even better idea to wait at least a year out of respect for the new spouse. All of us bring a certain amount of negative baggage to a marriage. Those who remarry late in life bring more – especially if they're recently widowed.

I heard of an 80-year-old widower who remarried four months after his wife's death. Apparently, his reputation for being impatient extended to his grieving process. I'm concerned for both of them.

Often I've confessed to members of support groups I've led: "If I were to find myself divorced or widowed, I'd probably do something thoroughly stupid out of loneliness." Because of this self-knowledge and being keenly aware of the value of friendships for those who are grieving, I've made a point of nurturing relationships with good friends. Because women generally maintain closer friendships than men, they are better equipped to handle the grieving process.

Valuing our independence does not necessarily mean we will want to remain single. It may mean we enter a new relationship with a greater sense of adventure, confidence, and, especially, wisdom. ❀

This Time Is for Me

I have come to Hawaii to watch the Wichita State Shocker baseball team play baseball with games on the Big Island at Kona and Hilo and then to the Rainbow Tournament on Oahu in Honolulu. It feels good to be here. I am here with old friends from Wichita. I will make new friends.

Is it right to be here? Of course. I came for me – the last time it was for Roy's memory. I was so lost, so bewildered. My grief still too new. Before returning home Kathy and Janis walked with me to the seaside at Waikiki. We prayed for Roy and I threw a white rose into the sea. Coming back here is like a beautiful reminder of our life together.

Getting here is not easy – six-hour flight from L.A. It makes for a long, long 12-hour day. And this year we flew in a very small plane with only six seats across in each row. I had a seatmate who coughed and blew his nose all the way. But he lives on the Big Island and was interesting to talk with – he spends his time in an outrigger. What a life!

And what a life I have. In the last few minutes the Shocks were robbed of a run at home plate, next batter hit to right field for a stand-up triple then Brandon Hill just hit a popup fly ball which was caught by the catcher and made our third out. We are in the bottom half of the third inning. We are in Hilo (first time to play here). It is cool with heavy clouds, a breezy wind and rain ready to pour at any minute.

Three days ago on my walk out the back door across the parking lot and through the greenhouse of the King Kameamea Hotel in Kona I practically bumped into a large bride's dress white butterfly enjoying the nectar from a row of some kind of beautiful pink flowers lining the rough path to the ballpark.

Each day I walked to the park along this back path around a wooded and flowering shortcut strewn with throwaways, plastic and useless, used up or forgotten pipe, lumber and concrete. Typical of Hawaii the back places hide what should be hauled to a dump but I don't think Hawaii has a solid waste dump. I hope it is not the sea.

It was the butterfly. A short, sweet presence flying around me while on its wider quest of nectar in preparation for life to come. It's also the symbol of Roy's presence that has come so often in unusual circumstances as to convince me they do not come by chance.

The same is true of the single-engine airplanes that fly over the ball fields. As we sat down in the bleachers at Kona and again just an hour ago along came the single-engine Cessna. Angels, if you will, reminding me I have never been without Roy's presence. Like the promise God made to leave us with God's Spirit no matter where or what. I have these three special symbols – butterfly, single-engine airplanes, mourning doves. At least one always seems to appear in my time of need.

I don't know how this works but I confess it happens at home as well as here in paradise or anywhere else I travel. But it is especially poignant to have that presence appear here again on this biennial trip to Hawaii to watch Roy's beloved Wichita State University Shocker baseball team play early season games where it is warm and inviting. The score is two to one in the bottom half of the fourth inning. Shocks are up.

Gene Blake reflects

There are many things in life we don't understand. Death is but one of them. How can a body with a vital presence and personality suddenly stop functioning? What happens to this spirit that has been such a significant part of our life? Can this spirit manifest itself in ways we don't quite comprehend and certainly can't prove?

Dr. Scott Peck in his book, *Further Along the Road Less Traveled*, defines four stages of spiritual growth. The fourth stage is being content to live with the mysteries of life – such as life and death. People joke that the three most difficult words for a man to utter are, "I don't know." The older I get the more I find myself respecting someone – male or female – who has the wisdom and courage to make that confession. Throughout the decades and centuries science may have explained many things that were inexplicable to our ancestors. However, some things transcend knowledge and definition.

I place death in that category. Why are we far more inclined to accept birth than death, particularly the death of a loved one? Since death is as normal and natural as birth why do we view it from an entirely different perspective?

I once met a woman who had a near death experience. I made a recording of my interview with her. What I remember most from our conversation was her complete lack of fear concerning death. In fact, she confessed she didn't want to return to life but preferred what was "on the other side." Mystery, it's there whether we accept it or deny it.

Turning to the Future

Subject: Sunday afternoon
Date: 3/29/2005 at 11:00 a.m.
From: Mom (Mimi in Kansas)
To: Shane and family in Texas

At 4 p.m. on Easter afternoon, Jason, Kristen and their girls, plus Steve and Sheryl and I met at your dad's grave side with Pastor Tom and his wife, Rev. Diane. They led us with an informal memorial/resurrection celebration for your dad. Tom played his guitar, we sang Amazing Grace, Diane read a story I had written in Hawaii two years ago.

Krystine had written a note to Papa and Jason's family brought red roses to place on the grave. Hannah and Krystine had special "we love you Papa" Mylar balloons which they released. As we watched the balloons catch the wind, the girls ran through the cemetery as if to chase their gifts to Papa up to heaven. A single-engine airplane flew over and then circled back around.

I had taken flowers to the grave on Wednesday, the 23rd, but it seemed very appropriate this year to have the short service on Easter Sunday, the 27th and third anniversary of the celebration of Roy's life and resurrection.

Grandma and Granddad Phillips decided they did not need to come – the family will gather with them for our annual Easter egg hunt next Sunday when Ron and Barbara return from a trip. Anne and Robert were with Bryce at a track meet.

The idea of a graveside gathering is a way for me of bringing closure to the intentional grief journey. It is symbolic pause between looking back while struggling to move forward and turning to face the future. I have grieved well for Roy. I may never be far from tears, in fact, my eyes moisten as I write this. But the wracking wretchedness is gone.

Any time when you are here, if you would like to have a brief service, I know Pastor would be glad to help us continue our journey.
I miss you all...
Love, Mom (Mimi in Kansas)

Gene Blake reflects

Have you seen the movie *About Schmidt*, starring Jack Nicholson? If not, consider renting the DVD. If you have, then you understand why someone like me (who'd reached his 65th birthday and whose daughter's wedding had recently occurred) shouldn't have watched it. Why? Because it deals with significant changes at these critical junctures of life. One might be tempted to over relate and go into depression. I managed to avoid it … barely.

Warren Schmidt, the character portrayed by Jack Nicholson, has to adjust to retirement, to the sudden death of his wife, to living alone, and to having his estranged daughter marry someone of whom he doesn't approve. Similar situations are faced by seniors every day. It may be another pill to take, an injury, a failed organ, chronic health problems, limited energy, giving up independence, the loss of a loved one … the list seems endless. Not long ago I joked to someone complaining about hip problems, "Isn't it fun to grow old and sit around waiting to see what's going to fall apart next?" It's no wonder older people have such a struggle with change: They (perhaps I should say we) have to deal with so much of it. I told someone recently, "I don't care what they say; I think 'change' is a four-letter word!"

Yet dealing with change is a lifelong struggle. Sometimes it's exciting and challenging. Sometimes it's a pain. To be human is to face a changing body, a changing identity, changing relationships, changing perspectives on life, or a changing environment. Even education involves change – it changes who we are. More than we realize we are constantly reinventing ourselves – particularly when we face overwhelming change like the loss of a spouse. The movie *About Schmidt* illustrates this quite well.

Hopefully, as we adjust to the constant changes throughout our life, we gain a little wisdom – we come to realize what is really important:
- human beings are not self-sufficient,
- family, friends, and church are needed support systems,
- people are more important than things, rules, and social customs,
- simple joys often outweigh significant accomplishments,
- doing something for another person is more rewarding than self-indulgence,

- our relationship to God is one of the few constants in life – even though how we view God may change.

Author Harold Kushner makes this observation: "When you have learned how to live, life itself is the reward." Learning how to live is a universal challenge – everyone has to deal with it. It's a life long process that transcends economic class and cultural background. And, if we've learned the lesson well, we've also learned the skills necessary to cope with the many and changing stages of our lives. On the one hand, we gain new skills, knowledge, and possibly even wisdom. On the other hand, as we age we have to accept increasing limitations. Learning how to live helps us to do both graciously and gracefully. That's our reward! ✿

We Remember Dad

Re: Sunday afternoon
Date: 3/29/2005 12:35 P.M.

Mom,
I'm glad the service was so nice. We have thought of Dad often lately. I told Shane his dad would love our new home and be very proud. We had our new 60" TV delivered and the cable hooked up with some extra features we didn't have at our old house. I know Dad would have loved watching a few games or movies with us on this fantastic equipment!

…the kids and I enjoyed a beautiful large black and yellow butterfly in the backyard yesterday. It was enjoying the purple phlox we have back there. It lingered drinking from the flowers for at least 15 minutes. Abby and I stood very close and just watched. The butterfly didn't seem to care that we were right there. I have never been so close to a butterfly for such a long period of time. I will send you a pic when I get them developed. The backyard is lovely right now with red and yellow tulips that have just opened. All the plants are getting new growth. Take care!
Love,
Shelley

Dedicated to Gardeners Everywhere

"Flowers seem intended for the solace of humanity."
John Ruskin

"If you would be happy all your life, plant a garden."
A Chinese Proverb

Rusty, rescued, red-metal lawn chair, white paint peeling,
waits as silent sentry on back deck.
Darkness retreats
Stars break camp
Dawn approaches
Day marches forth.
Seasons take control
Gray camouflages smell of spring
Blue sky captures summer
Green surrenders in fall to amber and rust
White drapes dead of winter
Time synchronizes cycles of living and dying.
Landscape mapped
Canarti junipers guard perimeter
Limestone boulders provide cover
Dandelions blossom.
New recruit orders
Join troops of sweat bees and army ants
Survey battle field
Surround henbit
Take out bindweed
Secure habitat for robin and wren
Troubleshoot irrigation lines

Provision mulch for grub, worm, and roly-poly
Halt advancement of Bermuda into Lantana territory
Sunder suckers surrounding Mountain Cherry
Guard against invasion of pine tip beetle
Deadhead daylily
Secure back-up troops to mow and fertilize.
But if this day you are
Too spent from duty in the summer sun
Too weary to take up arms of hoe and shears
Too sweaty and sore
Do not worry.
Languish in your junkyard chair
Refresh with ice tea.
Watch
Blue jays reconnoiter
Squirrels store hazel nuts and acorns
Forest Pansy Redbuds
Bindweed scale chain link fence
Butterflies sample nectar
Worms enrich soil
Rose of Sharon blossom
Hosta and Hydrangea recover.
Pause is received by Creation as praise
Pleased you pay attention
Deers eat apples
Army mules stop and talk
Mantis prays
Lady Bugs
Bumble bee z-z-z-z
Nature will not be defeated;
Neither will you.

Gene Blake reflects

There are life lessons to be found in the seasons of the year and the calendars that record them.
- Time not only marches on but, with a little help, can heal our physic wounds.
- Nature follows a cycle of birth, growth, vitality, decline, death, dormancy, and eventual renewal.
- In many ways, we can be co-creators with God by giving birth to the next generation, by nurturing children and grandchildren, and even by creating a place of beauty in our back yard.

Several years ago, I officiated at the committal service for a gardener who died at age 101. These are the comments I made at her graveside:

I just learned yesterday that Nettie and her late husband, David, loved to garden. I, too, share that interest. Perhaps it's no coincidence I'm reminded of a time this past September when I'd finished eating the last of my sweet corn and watermelon, blight had decimated my tomato vines, bugs were infesting the cantaloupe, weeds that had escaped me were going to seed; and I'd tired of gardening for the year. The thought struck me: How gardening is like life.

Spring, like birth and childhood, is a time of new life, great promise, and rapid growth. The summer months are a time of maturity, production, and harvest like our middle years. But fall brings withered vines, insects, diseases, and weeds – things not unlike the infirmities of old age. Not long ago I tilled up my garden – I returned its residue to the earth – just like today we return Nettie to the earth.

After several years of ministry I began to notice a phenomenon connected to the funerals at which I'd officiated. Almost invariably, there was a pregnant mother, baby, or young child in attendance. In a subtle way their presence made the point life goes on in its eternal cycles. The opening of my traditional prayer following the eulogy made the same point: "O God, before whom generations rise and pass away…"

About a decade ago, after we had built a new house and my landscaper/master gardener wife (with some help from me) had created rock embankments, a waterfall, pond, and numerous flower gardens, both my daughter and my spiritual director encouraged me to build a bench beside the pond so we could pause, rest, and enjoy what had been created. Well, I erected the bench, but I must confess I don't spend much time sitting on it. I've become too busy maintaining that beauty to enjoy it!

I commend Sherry for not only having her backyard – the place of Roy's death – newly landscaped, but also for the search she and my wife embarked upon to find an old metal lawn chair at an antique shop in Arkansas City – a chair where she can pause and observe the lessons of nature, and reflect on life.

Gene Blake writes

The Old Oak

For weeks I'd eyed the dead oak tree across the canyon when I went fishing at Chrisler's. Duane and Pat Chrisler were members of the church where I was pastor in Winfield and were good friends as well. Before his death, Duane built an 80-acre watershed lake on land he purchased decades ago from John Lowe. The lake has provided the best bass fishing I've ever enjoyed and the beauty of its shoreline trees and limestone cliffs are an escape to the solitude of nature.

Over nearly 20 years, driving to Chrisler's ranch became something of a ritual – like returning to my rural childhood. Sometimes it was to visit Duane and Pat, sometimes to fish small ponds Duane used for watering cattle, sometimes to hunt quail, sometimes to haul stone for our new house from their quarry near the watershed lake. And, for a few years, to take communion to John Lowe, who Pat cared for in a small stone house adjacent to their home.

John's wife died shortly after I came to Winfield. While officiating at her funeral I became acquainted with their son, Jim, who lived in Kansas City. Like Duane, Pat, and John, he, too, became a good friend. When I had major surgery at the University of Kansas Medical Center in Kansas City, Jim came to visit me as I'd visited his father many times. At the time John was well into his 90s and residing at the Presbyterian Manor nearby. Thinking of his father's age and health, Jim remarked, "We're going to have a funeral one of these days." A few months later there was a funeral – for 57-year-old Jim, not his father. Age and illness have since taken John and Duane. As with the old oak across the canyon vitality had given way to mortality.

With the advent of year's end and frosty mornings, it was time to cut firewood to fuel our fireplace – the one made of limestone from Chrisler's quarry. The old oak came to mind as I loaded chainsaws into my Ford Ranger. I drove east out of town and turned onto the gravel country road. I left the road for Chrisler's lane, bumped across a cattle guard, and took the fork in the road leading to the old John Lowe place. To my left was the canyon with limestone outcroppings on both sides. As the grass gave way to rocks and trees I searched for and found an exit from the poor excuse for a road. With the removal of a few small trees, I surmised my pickup could be backed close enough to save carrying pieces of the old oak up the hill. But first there was the task of dropping – in the right direction – a tree whose diameter was twice the length of my chainsaw – a tree whose branches reached like gnarled fingers 50 feet into the sky.

With chainsaw in hand I approached the tree as a warrior would approach a worthy adversary. Deeper in the canyon two white-tailed deer rattled dead leaves with their rapid retreat. With tails straight up they gave a graphic alarm my father would have likened to his white work mittens. As I approached the trunk of the old oak the sound of a tiny, trickling stream filled the quiet left by the deer. The source of the stream was a few yards up the canyon where an early settler had erected a circle of stones around a spring. Unlike the dead oak and surrounding trees, a few small oaks clung to leaves tastefully mingling burgundy with brown. Here and there bright red oak leaves conflicted with the color scheme. Further down the canyon ghostly white trunks of sycamore trees were exposed by the dropping of the leafy cover.

To control a tree's fall it's necessary to cut a notch that comes out in the desired direction. It's also helpful if the bulk of the tree points that direction along with the wind. This day I was lucky but not skillful. My notch was too big – the two cuts of my chainsaw were directed halfway through the tree. Hoping the sum of the cuts translated to several feet at the top of the dead oak, I began my cut on the other side just above my misguided notch. Ever so slowly the new cut widened as the tree began its descent. As the fibers snapped a little tremor of fear crept into my body. For a moment the trunk gripped my chainsaw and then with a crash the old oak parted company with its base and fell around me – in just the direction I wanted it to go. The canyon was silent again – no longer disturbed by the lion-like roar of my chainsaw, no longer echoing the crash of falling limbs.

Too tired to walk up the hill to my pickup, I began to count the rings in the trunk knowing each one represented a year's growth. Like a young child the wide inner rings showed rapid growth. The narrow outer rings, however, were difficult to discern in the rough sawn trunk. But they were there – 110 rings as best I could count – 110 years of growth and then death. What had the tree experienced in that time?

It didn't sprout until after Osage Indians traveled the Black Dog Trail nearby. Before it took root white settlers had made a home across the canyon – where they built rock fences and a cellar with walls and arched ceiling of limestone blocks. The oak's ancestors clung to the protection of the bends and banks of Silver Creek, where trees once found protection from prairie fires. But as the prairie at the edge of the Flint Hills was sacrificed to the plow, fires lost their source of fuel and trees like the old oak were freed to move from creek banks to canyons close by. The old oak had seen the near demise of wildlife such as deer and prairie chicken as settlers struggled to survive on the prairie. Soon Hereford cattle grazed its hillside. Yet the old oak lived long enough to see the deer return to its canyon once again. The brush at its base now provided places for bobcats to hide and its limbs welcomed turkeys for a nightly roost.

The old oak had outlived John Lowe with whom it almost shared a birthday. How many times had John admired this tree as he drove to his house? How many times, before his eyesight failed, before he sold the land to Chrisler's, before he died at age 97? The stone structures – the cellar, the fence, and the little wall around the spring – will remain for centuries until worn away by water and weather. The smaller oaks – like the old oak – will flourish for decades. But one day they too will die – just like John, Jim, and Duane. But this winter the old oak fuels my fireplace, bringing warmth to my home as memories of these men bring warmth to my heart. ✤

Testimony to Life

*"No ray of sunshine is ever lost,
but the green which it awakens into existence needs time to sprout,
and it is not always granted for the sower to see the harvest.
All work that is worth anything is done in faith."*
Landscape by Albert Schweitzer

My dear friend, Gene, has worked hard to teach me to pay attention. His story of The Old Oak is fruit of following that admonition. The lesson is practical and learnable. Valuable beyond price. Way too easy to ignore. But if we pause, watch and listen, there is reward.

Presence
Planted where found
Trunk with roots and limbs
Grown wide into the canyon's rocky soil
Stretching o u t
Reaching Up to ever changing sky
Rooted
Steadfast
Anchored
G
R
O
W
I
N
G
deep
Silent witness
Shelter
Present long after living
Remembered.

Tortoise Wins the Race of her Life

*The Hare was once boasting of his speed before the other animals.
"I have never yet been beaten," said he, "when I put forth my full speed.
I challenge any one here to race with me."
The Tortoise said quietly, "I accept your challenge."
…The Hare darted almost out of sight at once … The Tortoise plodded on and
plodded on … Then said the Tortoise: "Plodding wins the race."*
AESOP D564 B.C.

*In darkness before dawn
she rises to pray
the only way
possible.
Bare feet turn east
God she cannot greet
out loud.
With thanks
for sky above
and earth below,
her feet
step out
on faith
one foot in front of the other,   one step at a time.
Her promise –
stay close to earth
take care of self
look up, see light
love everyone you meet
give thanks
for each new day.
Her faith filled actions do not go unnoticed.*

Perseverance

As I gather this collection of my experiences and reflections accumulated along my journey, I am aware the trek has no end. Oh, the hardest part, I believe, has passed. Even as I celebrate my survival I regret the necessity to have had to start down that unmarked road.

I will always miss Roy – the habits of our life together – and I sometimes resent the new routines that have replaced them as I live alone. But I am not lonely. I have new friends. I have traveled to new places – Alaska and Thailand. I still do one new thing each year I have never done before. Even gaining confidence in most things financial. I feel as secure as one can be. Roy's planning provided bedrock for me to build on in his absence. And I am grateful.

Death continues to capture loved ones and gives opportunity to persevere, to keep plodding. As always the timetable is unpredictable. I am willing to make the adjustments of being old. Hannah and Derek have invited me to live with them. Now that is a blessing!

The beauty of the earth is the focus of my enjoyment for and appreciation of life itself.

My grandchildren, now numbering five with AnnMarie added to Jason and Kristen's family, keep me younger than my years. They invite me for makeovers and manicures. They have their own curiosity about the Papa they never had a chance to know well or long. I still call them my Donut Hole Gang. They each one make me proud and Roy would be delighted how much they are like us. Shane and Jason are preparing to be patriarchs of the clan. They can handle it I have no doubt.

Because of my long history of living with Type 1 diabetes I am now part of the Joslin Diabetes Center 50-year Medalist Study which will receive the donation of part of my organs when I draw my last breath. A privilege received with a grateful heart.

I share my testimony of these timeless events and pray there are ears that will hear and eyes that can see my growing in this Landscape of Life.

About the Authors

Sherry Phillips' career as homemaker, wife, and mother of two sons was complemented by a thirty-year commitment as a Presbyterian Church (U.S.A.) elder to work for justice and peace in the global community with emphasis on women and children.

Her writing experience focused on interpretation and organization. Reports on meetings and events were written from her personal perspective and reflected a desire to engage others in a commitment to peacemaking. She expressed her feelings and experiences through a newsletter she produced for six years for area churches, letters to the editors of local newspapers, poetry about her grandchildren, and creative non-fiction pieces published in church newsletters.

Sherry traveled to Europe three times including a trip to the U.S.S.R. in 1983 participating in dialogue with others seeking peace. She made presentations to a variety of groups across the region to engage the thinking of others and arouse pursuits for justice. A trip to Thailand provided an opportunity to observe the overwhelming poverty and challenge that still faces too much of the world.

Rev. Eugene Blake's employment history started in his teen years as he worked on ranches near his home. For fourteen years – most of them as a registered professional engineer – he was employed in engineering, sales, and marketing. Becoming a church school teacher and youth group sponsor led not only to three youth mission trips to Mexico, but also to his enrolling in the University of Dubuque Theological Seminary.

Following ordination as a minister in the Presbyterian Church (U.S.A.), he served churches in Iowa and Kansas. In addition to usual pastoral duties, while at First Presbyterian Church, Winfield, Kansas, he led a bereavement support group co-sponsored by Cowley County Hospice. When he was president of the board of directors of that organization, the decision was made to merge with what was to become Harry Hynes Memorial Hospice in Wichita, Kansas.

In retirement, Gene has pursued yet another vocation: writing. He has written freelance articles for a number of agricultural publications, but primarily for Meredith Corp.

Made in the USA
Lexington, KY
26 October 2019